C000263067

Published by Intel Springs 2014

Copyright ©

Foluke Sangobowale has asserted her right under the Copyright, Designs and Patents Act 1988 to be identified as the author of this work.

First published in Great Britain in 2014

ISBN 978-0-9926385-0-4

Due to the dynamic nature of the internet, any web addresses or links contained in this book may have changed since publication and may no longer be valid.

Table of Contents

Acknowledgement

Firstly, I would like to thank God for His inspiration and for the opportunity He has given me to follow my dream of positively impacting lives.

I am grateful to my husband Ayodeji for encouraging me to write this book. To my wonderful children Tobi aged 11, Tito aged 8 and Demilade aged 5; thank you for your love and encouragement. You're the best. You inspire me daily to keep pressing on. It's not over until you win. Without you I would not have had the opportunity to write this book.

I express my appreciation to Pastors Matthew and Yemisi Ashimolowo for their Ministry and inspiration. I am indebted to the beautiful Mrs Yemisi Akindele, for her mentorship, guidance and re-assurances through my 11+ journey with my son. I wish to thank my big brother Dr Akinyemi Ajayi for his unwavering support and love. To Bree and Nikky, thanks so much for your help and support.

Lastly, for all their relentless love, prayers and encouragement, I would like to express thanks to my supportive parents Mr Alexander Ajayi J.P & Mrs Florence Ajayi J.P.

Introduction

WHY I WROTE THIS BOOK

"Expectations of children are "far too low" in Comprehensive schools and must be brought up to the standard of private and Grammar schools, the Head of OFSTED[1] said today".- Telegraph (UK) 13 June 2013

"Thousands of bright children are being "systematically failed" by England's non-selective secondaries, education inspectors warn". - Reported by bbc.co.uk 13 June 2013

There is a popular saying that knowledge is power. I decided to write this book to ensure that parents have the right information to provide their child with the best platform for secondary school education. The 11+ examination determines what type of secondary education a child would have. It's the prerequisite for gaining entrance into Year 7 at top UK Grammar schools and top UK Independent schools. Year 7 is the first year of secondary school. I am convinced that the earlier parents start to plan and prepare for this 11+ journey, the easier and more realistic it becomes to achieve the goal. The fierce competition for places at these top UK schools means that if a child is to secure a place, they must be thoroughly ready for the 11+ exams. The process involves revising for the exams over a long period to guarantee that the preparation is consistent and constant.

My aim is to enlighten parents about the 11+ exams and the process involved in applying for Grammar and Independent schools in the UK. A number of parents place immense importance on the 11+ exam because it is seen as a way to ensure that their child attends schools that offer a better chance of an admission to a good University. Parents need this information because there are few Grammar and Independent school places and a seemingly infinite number of people who want to get in. Therefore, there is tough competition for the available places. The first chapter explains exactly what 11+ exams are and why a lot of parents now choose this education route for their child. Let me make it crystal clear, I don't have anything against Comprehensive schools at all, but when I hear comments that regulators such as the Office for Standards in Education (OFSTED), are releasing into the public domain, it gives me great concern. However, it's well documented and there is overwhelming evidence that the Grammar and Independent school route offers many children so much more in their educational attainment hence my reason for being an 11+ supporter.

My aim is to provide answers to a lot of crucial questions that parents usually ask regarding the whole 11+ process. As parents embark on reading this book, I really hope that they will be able to find vital pointers that can ease their path through the 11+ process.

Some of my associates have asked me what I think about the 11+ process and some have expressed their confusion about where to even begin their preparation. I observed from the questions they asked that there are still many parents out there who, through no fault of their own, aren't aware of the rigour of 11+ exams. Many parents already find the process of helping their child transition to secondary school daunting and long-winded. The 11+ process only adds to this confusion. I experienced the same parental anxieties when I was faced with the realities of my son's transition into secondary education. Having experienced the 11+ process with my son, I feel the need to help other parents realise that this process allows pupils to become high achievers regardless of their socio-economic background.

This book provides the essential information needed by parents to make good choices about schools for their child. It gives an explanation of the grades chart on a child's end of the year school report. I have outlined the important steps that parents should follow to achieve success. These steps are proven to have worked for many families that have had 11+ successes.

Personally, when I first realised the tasks involved in the 11+ process, I panicked because it all seemed like a complex process to comprehend.

I wasn't sure if I wanted my son to take the exams or if he could cope with the hard work involved. It is often said that the state education system in the UK is intended to teach most children to be average. The 11+ process comes with a different agenda, it is about making children operate at a higher level and attain a better education. My experience of the process was dramatic at times as I was not an informed mum at the time. My aim is to enlighten other parents so that they don't end up going through some of the challenges of 11+ that I went through.

For parents intending to send their child to a local Comprehensive secondary school, this book will still be useful in providing a balanced view of the different types of secondary school education in the UK. Children attending Comprehensive schools are not required to sit 11+ exams. This book also contains advice to parents on factors to consider when choosing the right school for their child.

I do understand that families are facing challenging times and worry about the affordability of Independent schools. Obviously this point will be at the back of their mind while considering the type of secondary school education to choose for their child. School fees associated with Independent schools have been a major factor deterring many parents from even considering this option. Therefore, I will also give an outline of the types of financial assistance available to parents to help with private education school fees. I have since discovered that a lot of parents are uninformed about the support available through bursaries, scholarships and grants awarded by Independent schools and charitable trusts.

My aim is to demystify the process behind 11+ and the entry to Grammar and Independent schools. It is my sincere wish to help parents believe that this goal is achievable through hard work and dedication. I don't intend to dictate to parents which schools to choose for their child but to offer assurances that it is possible for a child to attend a top UK school even if their parents are not wealthy. I will not be making any recommendation of schools in this book because I wouldn't want to usurp the role of the parents reading this book. I want to give parents the opportunity to carry out their independent research about appropriate schools and make informed choices about schools without any undue influence. I will however help with the process by giving details of where information on schools can be freely and readily accessed.

Parent Tips:

• Please invest in a diary or a calendar as there are many dates you will need to make a note of as I take you through the journey of the 11+ process. Parents will be required to make a note of when 11+ exams registration process begins with the Local Education Authority (LEA) or with the Independent and Grammar schools. You will need to make a note of deadlines for application submission, exam dates, scholarship exam dates for Independent schools, deadlines to apply for bursaries and scholarships...there are just too many dates to try to cram into the brain.

- For ease of reference, I have included a table of UK's primary school age and class guide. I have made a lot of references to age and year groups throughout this book. Therefore, this table should be helpful mainly to those parents who are unfamiliar with the UK's Primary school education system.

UK's primary school age and class guide

Age	Year group or class group
Age 4 to 5	Reception Year
Age 5 to 6	Year 1
Age 6 to 7	Year 2
Age 7 to 8	Year 3
Age 8 to 9	Year 4
Age 9 to 10	Year 5
Age 10 to 11	Year 6

Overseas Students

Overseas students attending UK's top fee-paying schools have reached unprecedented levels. They are subject to the ever-changing immigration rules. It is important for overseas parents who are interested in the UK's education system, to make themselves familiar with these rules published by the United Kingdom's Home Office. It's imperative that parents familiarise themselves with their preferred school's admissions criteria as well. The current immigration rule is that overseas applicants under the age of 16 should only apply to fee-paying Independent schools for study. State-funded Grammar schools are only able to accept overseas candidates between 16 and 17 years old and ready to start their 'A' levels. A child is able to attend a state-funded school if they are under the age of 16 only if the child is coming for a short exchange or educational visit. Most Independent schools give overseas applicants written tests in Maths and English to gauge their ability. In addition to taking the entrance exams, interviews are also arranged by some of the schools. If a child is found to be attending a state-funded school other than for a short exchange or educational visit, they will infringe the immigration rules and action could be taken against them by the United Kingdom Border Agency.

'Independent' Grammar schools like Bristol Grammar School are able to accept overseas or international students from when they are in Year 7 up to A' Levels stage because it's a school that is not state-funded. This is explained further in chapter 3. Such schools usually require parents who are not UK residents, to appoint a suitable UK resident Guardian for their child, before an acceptance letter is sent to the applicant.

"Education is the most powerful weapon which you can use to change the world."

-Nelson Mandela

CHAPTER 1
What is the 11+ entrance exam?

The 11+ examination determines what sort of education a child could go on to. The fact is that those who excel in it have the opportunity of a Grammar school education while those who don't rarely get that opportunity. The term 11+ comes from the age group for secondary school entry which is 11 years. 11+ exams facilitate the admission process to various UK Grammar schools and Independent schools. Pupils that wish to gain entrance into a UK Grammar school must sit and pass these 11+ exams normally taken in Year 6 which is the last year of primary school. Children who wish to gain entrance to some selective UK Independent schools also sit 11+ style tests referred to as Common Entrance exams.

For ease of clarity, I will refer to the exams taken for both Grammar schools and Independent schools as the 11+ exams throughout this book. To put things into perspective, I will later explain the differences between the varying types of secondary school education available in the UK e.g. Grammar, Independent and Comprehensive schools.

To gain entrance into a Grammar school, the exams required vary between different schools, Counties and Local Education Authorities (LEAs). Similarly, 11+ exam styles vary between Independent schools. As a result of this variation, it is advisable to prepare a child for all the exams' main subject combinations which are Maths, English, Verbal Reasoning and Non-Verbal Reasoning.

Grammar schools and Independent schools offer a good quality education not offered by a lot of Comprehensive schools. A lot of parents have misunderstood the concept of the 11+. A good number of children like my son actually sit the exams when they are age 10+ at the beginning of Year 6. However, a lot of children are already 11 years old when the exam is taken. In my experience, a lot of parents have been oblivious to this piece of information and have missed a crucial opportunity for their child as a result. I recently met a parent who assumed that 11+ exams are taken when children are in Year 7. Another parent only became aware of the process two weeks prior to the 11+ exam and therefore did not have enough time to prepare her child.

Pupils have only one chance to sit 11+ exams and there is no opportunity to re-sit if the exam is failed. This is why I repeatedly reminded my son to "get on with it" whenever he was slacking with his revision. My favourite words to him were "Listen son! This is your only opportunity and you'd better not mess up".

The 11+ exams tests a candidate's ability and capacity to solve problems using Mathematics and reasoning skills as well as their English skills - grammar, punctuation, vocabulary and spelling. The 11+ process is certainly a test of persistence, determination and perseverance. Competition for Grammar schools is fierce due to the fact that the demand for space outnumbers supply. The truth is that not all children can handle this process. Parents have to make a judgment call about the decision to encourage their child to sit the exam.

The 11+ process involves a lot of pressure on the child and the parents. It is very daunting and successfully getting through the exams takes a lot of hard work, self-motivation, dedication and determination by the child as well as the parents. It is all about teamwork. Parents need to make up their minds if they choose to pursue this education route and be determined to take the bull by the horns. Parents will need to stand firm on their decisions as they may be faced with a lot of people trying to dissuade them from the process with comments such as "all schools are the same", "why bother with a Grammar school, what's the point?", "why waste your time and energy on 11+?"

Parents need to be 100% sure of what they would like to achieve from this process and not jump on the bandwagon just because other children are taking the exams. If the parents' aim is for their child to achieve their potential and go to a school that will challenge them and bring out the best in them then by all means they should get involved in the 11+ process.

The most important thing about education is appetite."-

-Winston Churchill

CHAPTER 2
My experience as an 11+ Mum and the 'winning' conversation

My experience as an 11+ Mum

My obsession with 11+ before my son sat the exam is indescribable. I realised after a while that I was not alone and many 11+ parents were in the same situation as me. Although I always appeared calm and regularly reassured myself that my son had done enough revision to pass, deep within, I was fearful and worried that he would fail. I couldn't sleep well at times because I was stressing about the 11+ exams and how well my son would be able to cope. I was fearful of the competition out there. I have to say that I was definitely more stressed about it than my husband.

11+ did not really take over his time the way it took over mine. I was so nervous about the whole process but masked my feelings from everyone except from my son's tutor who understood exactly how I felt. I was anxious about the amount of work and revision involved. I had so many questions on my mind. Will he be well physically on the day of the exam? Will he be able to answer all the questions within the allocated time? Will he excel and pass with flying colours?

Due to the fear factor, I got stuck into the process so that I could learn more about the level of knowledge required to excel in 11+ subjects such as Maths, Verbal Reasoning, Non-Verbal Reasoning and English. In the process, I familiarised myself with 11+ test papers as if I were the one sitting the exams. I approached everyone I knew of, whose child had sat the 11+ and I shamelessly asked countless questions about the process. I took necessary bold steps to complete and submit my Masters dissertation six months earlier so that I could have enough time to spend revising with my son for his 11+. I knew all the answers to 11+ revision papers without needing the help of the answer booklets. I learnt a lot of short cuts that were useful in answering questions quicker. I was able to pass this knowledge to my son.

I bought many revision resources - half of which my son did not even use. I did a thorough research on both Grammar and Independent schools and did not jump on the bandwagon of picking schools that were popular with other parents. I did my own independent research of schools that would accommodate my son's unique abilities.

There is a popular adage that education is not only a ladder of opportunity, but also an investment in our future. Our children are our future. Many parents have shown interest in the 11+ process and have asked me for advice. Some have asked why I decided to send my son to a Grammar school. My own educational background is probably one of the main reasons.

I was given a good education and I feel the need to do even better for my children. In my quest for knowledge, I registered and participated in some 11+

online parent forums but later de-registered myself as I found some of these forums to be occasionally useful but scaremongering at times.

I showed interest in my son's work and made sure that revision was not a lonely experience for him. He had a stable routine as I helped him add structure to his revision timetable. I was prepared for occasional mood swings and tantrums and would curtail these before they even began. I watched his diet ensuring that there was less sugar in his daily intake to help his concentration skills. Nearer the 11+ exams, I ensured he had a good night's sleep before waking him up for some early morning revision before heading off to school.

Overall, I feel elated that my son excelled in his exams and gained admission into one of UK's top Grammar schools. However, I am more grateful that this experience has given me the opportunity to be able to help other parents gain the knowledge they require to fulfil the ambition they have for their child.

The 'Winning' Conversation
Some parents tell their child "Son it's not about winning, it's about taking part". Well, I say the reverse "Son, it's not just about taking part, it's about winning". I believe that this is the mind-set that parents should equip their children with if they are going to enter into this 11+ race. It is a competition and the race is not for the weak.

Having a Winning Mentality
As parents it is necessary to instil in a child, the willingness to succeed. Success in any sphere of life, calls for one to adopt a positive mental attitude and to take full responsibility for one's life. Parents should advise their children not to apportion blame to others for lack of success. They should always look at ways of getting better in any subject they are finding difficult. Children should

be given the opportunity to devise plans for overcoming those obstacles. Encourage the child to visualise their goals and sharpen the skills they have in order to attain those goals.

Parent Tip:

Don't let your children be ordinary when they can be extra-ordinary. I say to parents, success is at your fingertips and all you have to do is reach out, believe, work hard and grasp what is rightfully yours.

CHAPTER 3
What are Grammar, Independent and Comprehensive Schools?

Many parents have asked me this question and I feel this is a perfect opportunity to provide clarity on the different terminologies used to describe the different types of schools and to explain the different features of these schools. In the UK, secondary schools are usually grouped into Grammar schools, Independent schools and Comprehensive schools. In order to make things clearer, I have endeavoured to offer an explanation of these three main types of mainstream secondary schools in the UK.

GRAMMAR SCHOOLS
There are 164 Grammar schools in the UK[2]. Most of these schools are state-funded[3] schools that select their pupils by means of the 11+ exam set by the LEA, the County or the school itself. It is widely known that most of these Grammar schools are in the following Counties; Buckinghamshire, Lincolnshire, Essex, Slough, Surrey, Kent, Gloucestershire and Trafford in Manchester. In most cases, parents do not have to pay school fees however, if

parents choose to send their child to a boarding[4] Grammar school, they may have to pay for the boarding facility. Also, parents need to be aware of the fact that there are a few 'Independent' Grammar schools like Manchester Grammar School that charge fees of up to £10,000 per annum. The main features of such Independent Grammar schools are that as well as being highly academically selective, they also charge high school fees. Some parents might think that fees are not charged in such schools as these schools also have the word 'Grammar' included in their school name. Parents are advised to check whether their preferred Grammar school is a non-fee paying state Grammar school or a fee paying one.

Grammar schools are often referred to as selective schools because their pupils are chosen based on the academic ability shown through the 11+ exams. Apart from the 11+ exams set by the LEA, some Grammar schools like Reading Boys Grammar school choose to set their own entry tests and only admit children who succeed in these. Admission to a preferred Grammar school is not guaranteed, even if a candidate has excelled in the 11+ exams. All Grammar schools have their admissions oversubscription criteria which they use to allocate places if they receive more applications than the places they have available.

Children who do not sit the 11+ Grammar school exams have the option of attending a Comprehensive school and also have the option of sitting the 11+ entrance exams for Independent schools.

I am aware of the fact that there are many bright children that don't actually sit 11+ because their parents are concerned about the competitiveness as well as the cost involved in tutoring. People have criticised the fact that Grammar schools often create a divide and do not offer equal opportunity to all children to have the same model of education. It is widely suggested that Grammar schools are mainly for children from middle class families as these families are the ones able to afford the intensive tutoring needed to excel in 11+ exams. I know that this is not always the case as parents have the option of purchasing resources and self-tutoring their child. The application process for most Grammar schools is free, unlike that of Independent schools.

INDEPENDENT SCHOOLS

Independent schools are also referred to by some as Private or Public schools. Independent schools generate their own funding from a variety of sources such as tuition fees, private grants, alumni association and fundraising from parents and the community. A number of people use the words Independent school, Public school and Private school interchangeably so it has become quite confusing. The distinguishing factor is that these schools are not state-funded therefore they charge steep fees. While some people assume that teachers at Comprehensive schools are as qualified as those at Independent schools, it is important to note that some Independent schools that focus on academic achievements may prefer to hire a teacher with a PhD.

The school fees range from about £4,000 to £12,000 per term. However, some help may be available towards the fees and I will discuss the issue of bursaries, grants and scholarships in subsequent chapters. Most Independent schools use 11+ selection processes to admit pupils into Year 7 and they also request a Head Teacher's report from a child's primary school. This report helps them decide if a child is suitable for admission to their school.

I personally know of a number of parents who previously assumed that they could never afford Independent school fees but they eventually found themselves turning to these Independent schools when their children could not gain admission into Grammar schools. They were forced into taking this major decision to prevent their child attending a non-performing local Comprehensive state school.

Independent schools are an expensive option for many, but parents should not panic. As mentioned earlier, the chapter on financial assistance provides an insight into the financial options like bursaries and scholarships available to families. It's like taking out a mortgage. Parents will have to research the various Independent schools and make an informed decision about their preferences. Parents have to ensure that they will get value for their investment! Some very oversubscribed Independent schools close their application process about two years prior to proposed entry for 11+. In such situations, no further registrations will be accepted when a sufficient number of applications for any particular year have been received.

There are different categories of Independent schools. Some are described as 'Public schools', a term usually associated with Independent, exclusive and older fee-paying secondary schools that were established in some cases, well over 400 years ago. Schools such as Winchester College and Eton College fall into this category. Only a few of these 'Public' schools take pupils from the age of 11. The majority of them take their pupils from the age of 13 when a child is in Year 9. The Independent Schools Examination Board (ISEB) UK sets 11+ Common Entrance exams and 13+ entrance exams for some of these Public schools. Candidates wishing to apply for scholarship at such schools might have to take a separate Scholarship exam paper in addition to the Common Entrance papers. Parents are able to contact any Public school directly for their prospectus or contact ISEB for details of the admissions process. The Scholarship exam is tougher than the Common Entrance Exam as its aim is to identify the most intelligent and gifted candidates and entice them with an offer of a fee reduction.

If parents wish to follow the Independent school route, especially targeting the public schools, it is advisable they register their child at a good Preparatory school at a very early age. A number of these Preparatory schools are feeder schools for some really good Independent 'Public' secondary schools. I will explain what feeder schools are in the next section.

Some years ago, I was advised by associates that the only way to gain a place in some oversubscribed Independent secondary schools was to register my child's birth and head straight to the highly sought after feeder school, to put his name on the school's waiting list. To my horror, I soon found out that some parents actually timed the birth of their child so that they could gain priority on such school's waiting list. Let me elaborate on this point. Basically, my child was born in August and the amusing thing is that babies born in July or August have a slimmer chance of getting a place at such schools as all the spaces would have been taken by children born in the autumn and winter months. This is not an exaggeration!

A lot of parents choose to educate their child at Independent schools for a variety of reasons. The general opinion is that some Independent schools offer a broad range of extra-curricular activities. It's a fact that some of their buildings are admired for being grand, very attractive and a good number of these schools offer very high academic standards and have good world-wide reputation.

What is a Feeder School or a Preparatory School?
A feeder primary school works in conjunction with a secondary or Grammar school within a catchment area in order to facilitate the admission of pupils in

that school upon reaching secondary school age. This means that the primary school is linked to or feeds into a designated secondary school.

These smaller primary or preparatory schools that send their graduating pupils to an affiliated secondary level school are called 'feeder' schools. For obvious reasons, a place in one of these feeder schools increases a child's likelihood of entering an oversubscribed secondary school.

Application process - Independent school

The application process varies between different Independent schools. As an 11+ mum, the general advice that I was given was to apply in the Autumn term two years before my son was intending to sit the exams for the school, this is so that my son has ample time to get ready for the main entrance exam. For example we were advised to apply around November 2011 for a place in September 2013.

Parents must ensure that the application forms are obtained, completed and returned to the preferred Independent school with the registration fee, if any, within the specified deadlines. Most Independent schools charge a non-refundable registration fee for their 11+ entry. Registration means that a child will be invited for 11+ entry tests and an interview in the year before their proposed entry.

In my experience, I found that the registration fees per school range from between £50 - £300. This amount could easily stack up if parents are considering applying to a number of Independent schools. Usually registration fees are paid directly to the school either online or by cheque when the application forms are returned. Some schools do not accept late applications.

The Interview – Independent school

Many Independent secondary schools set their own 11+ entrance exams for entry to Year 7 and they are not all monitored by ISEB. Their entrance exams usually consist of English, Maths, Creative Writing, Verbal Reasoning and Non-Verbal Reasoning. Independent schools would normally invite a child that has excelled in the entry tests for an interview. The schools are usually looking for evidence of neat written work, fluency in reading, competent level of spelling and grammar. Interviews for Independent schools come in different forms. At times they may involve a formal interview with the Head Teacher or with the Head of Year 7. These interviews could involve a child having to meet with and be interviewed by a panel of senior staff members as well. They might be asked to discuss, for example, their sporting achievements or talk about their general achievement portfolio. There are some Independent schools that request candidates to bring with them something of which they are particularly proud as well as their primary school English and Maths work books.

Independent 'Public' school - Common Entrance exams

Independent Secondary schools that have Public school status usually hold Common Entrance 11+ and 13+ exams. These exams are set by ISEB with the aim of selecting candidates that are deemed most suitable. Some feeder or preparatory Independent schools have syllabuses that are developed and regularly monitored by ISEB. The 11+ entrance exams usually consist of papers in Maths, Science, English and Creative Writing.

These 11+ and 13+ exams are for entry to Year 7 and Year 9 of some super-selective Independent schools like the UK's prestigious Eton College and Harrow School. The 13+ exam paper usually covers subjects such as English, Science, Maths, Geography, History and Languages. Some schools require that candidates also choose a foreign language as one of their options. These schools offer places based on how well applicants perform in the gruelling interview process they also assess the reference received from an applicant's current school. ISEB allows preparatory or feeder schools to teach almost all its pupils to a common syllabus and the marking of the exam papers and the admissions process is facilitated by each Public school.

The general myth is that Independent schools are less rigid in their selection process than Grammar schools as they are only interested in money making. This is not always true. Some of these 'super selective' and very oversubscribed schools would only choose children who perform highly in their entrance exams. A school is usually described as 'oversubscribed' when the number of students applying to the schools out-numbers the amount of spaces available in the school.

I would suggest that parents thoroughly carry out their research on each preferred school to ensure that these schools are performing very well academically and would offer a well–rounded education to their child. Parents should also check the admissions criteria and not be misled by all the façade that some Independent schools have. Grandiose buildings which slightly justify some of the ridiculously high school fees are not always a sign of academic strength and it is advisable not to make such an assumption.

COMPREHENSIVE SCHOOLS

Comprehensives are state funded secondary schools for children between the ages of 11 to 18. For this reason, they are also known as 'State' schools. These schools do not generally select pupils based on academic ability.

It is widely described by many as a system in which pupils of all abilities are educated together. There is a caveat to this point. Generally in the UK, most of the really good Comprehensive schools are very 'oversubscribed' and usually have an admissions criteria. For a child to have a good chance of gaining admission to such schools, usually they must be residing within the catchment area of the school.

The general advice is that pupils can apply for state schools outside their local council area however; their application has to be processed through the LEA where they reside at the time of the application.

During the application process, some Comprehensive schools select a certain number or percentage of pupils on the basis of e.g. aptitude for Sport or Music. Some schools also have specialism in subjects such as Arts, Languages, ICT[5] and Mathematics and parents should take into account their child's area of specialism if any, when choosing schools. It will be beneficial if parents have a discussion with their child before making a final decision on school choices. There is more information in subsequent chapters about the application process to the LEA.

It is a fact that most of the top Comprehensive schools in the UK are situated in affluent areas which therefore make them inaccessible to children from poorer backgrounds. It is not uncommon for parents from less affluent backgrounds to rent homes in these expensive, affluent areas just to try and secure a place at these schools.

Parents beware! In the last few years, the number of investigations into fraudulent and suspicious school applications has been regularly debated. I am aware of the fact that local councils usually query applications if there are concerns about parents using fake addresses and documentation to obtain admission. It is a known fact that some local authorities have in the past withdrawn fraudulently obtained admissions. It is unfair for any child to be put through such traumatic experience.

In the last few years, there has been a lot of debate about under performance of some Comprehensive schools. Recent reports released by the education regulators about Comprehensive schools have been scalding. OFSTED's report highlighted that; "based on observations of 2,000 lessons, visits to 41 schools and school performance data, in some non-selective schools, teachers did not know who their most able pupils were. In 40% of the schools visited, the brightest students were not making the progress of which they were capable, and many had become 'used' to performing at lower levels, with parents and teachers accepting this 'too readily'- OFSTED" Reported by bbc.co.uk 13 June 2013.

Parent Tips:

• Find out about your preferred school's admissions process as early as possible so that you can adequately prepare for it.

• Every child is unique and has their own talent; therefore it is advisable not to copy other parents' decisions. Parents need to think independently about choice of schools and consider factors such as finances, the educational and social needs of a child, distance from home etc. The key advice is to 'do your research'.

CHAPTER 4
Why send a child to a Grammar school or an Independent school?

Every year, the league table of schools proves that Grammar and Independent schools produce excellent results in GCSEs and A'levels in comparison to a lot of Comprehensive schools. Year on year, many of the schools featured on the published 'Top 100' list of best UK schools are Grammar and Independent schools. This is the reason why many parents still strive to send their child to such selective schools. A high number of the students that these schools produce also make progress to Russell group[6] universities in the UK as well as Ivy league[7] universities in the United States of America.

The role of their academic teachers is to ignite imagination and a passion for learning in all their pupils. The pupils have the opportunity to travel extensively and are more confident in their abilities. Such an education broadens a child's horizon and ultimately helps with networking in the future. Grammar and Independent schools build important skills and enthusiasm in children and help develop personality characteristics such as resilience, concentration and teamwork which are all important skills to have. A high number of Comprehensive schools are under-performing and the threat of closure hangs over a lot of these schools. The recent statement made by OFSTED confirms that.

It is a known fact that employers place high value on extra-curricular activities that pupils are involved in while at school. Grammar schools and Independent schools offer so many of these activities such as the Duke of Edinburgh's Award[8]. This award gives a lot of pupils the chance to develop important work and life skills that are highly valued by employers. Many of the extra-curricular activities present opportunities for pupils to represent their schools in a wide variety of competitions.

Parent Tips:

• The best school for your child is a highly personal decision based on your income, family, your values and most importantly, the needs, talents and interests of your child.

• Parents, be alert! There are a number of state Grammar schools that are now classed as Independent schools and they charge high school fees. Parents can be misled as these schools also have the word 'Grammar' included in their school name.

CHAPTER 5
What subjects are taken at 11+ and What is CEM (Centre for Evaluation and Monitoring) 11+?

WHAT SUBJECTS ARE TAKEN AT 11+?

The main subjects that children sit for Grammar school and Independent schools 11+ exams are Maths, English, Reasoning tests which comprise Verbal Reasoning (VR), Non-Verbal Reasoning (NVR) and Creative Writing. Grammar schools allocate places depending on a pupil's results in these 11+ exams. Subjects taken vary between different LEAs, Grammar schools, Independent schools and counties but the nature of the exams will constitute some or all of the subjects mentioned above. It is therefore advisable to check the exact details of subjects to be examined with the relevant LEA, County, Grammar or preferred Independent schools.

There are usually two different types of exam format to the Maths and English papers. It is important to check with the LEA or the schools if the exams will be in either multiple choice or standard format.

Multiple-Choice Format

This is where pupils have to select the answer from a separate answer sheet. The right answer will have to be chosen out of about five or more options.

Standard Format

With the standard format Maths exams for instance, candidates will have to show the workings on the examination booklet provided. There is usually space beneath the question and a child is required to write or work out their answer in that space. It would surely help if parents were able to obtain revision resources similar to the format which will be taken in the main exam as this would help the child to familiarise themselves with the exam format.

CEM 11+

There is a new CEM 11+ test which LEAs, some Grammar and Independent schools have introduced in the past few years to combat the problem of children being highly tutored for 11+. I will go into more details on CEM 11+ later on in this chapter.

Maths

The minimum Maths level expected for 11+ exams is Key stage 2 levels 4-6. A child taking the 11+, needs to be up to speed with times tables, metrics and the basic elements of Maths. The Maths exam is usually a non-calculator exam paper therefore it is necessary for pupils to be top notch in mental maths as this will help with the speed required to complete the exams. The main topics that are covered include: angles, probability, co-ordinates, charts, trigonometry, algebra etc. This list is not exhaustive, it is important that parents check the LEA's exam syllabus or past question papers of their preferred Grammar or Independent school. This will provide a good indication of previously asked questions.

Usually the time allowed for this exam varies between 35–60 minutes for possibly 30 to 50 Maths questions. Therefore, it is important for a child to practice prudent ways of reaching the right answer, as speed and accuracy are essential skills to have.

Examples of 11+ Maths questions are shown below:

- 56% of the population prefer Football to Rugby. What percentage of the population prefers Rugby to Football?

- Six ball pens cost £37.20. How much will eight of the same ball pens cost?

- A number multiplied by itself gives the answer 49. Circle the number from the options given. 2 3 4 5 6 7 8 9

- 213 216 219 222 225 Write down the next two terms of the number sequence.

- What is 105 days in weeks?

- What is 3450 millilitres in litres?

 **Parent Tips:** You can test your child's mental Maths skills as they sit in the back of the car, at the dining table and as you walk to the shop with them. Make learning fun for them; teach them lots of Maths tips if you are aware of any. Get your child to practice lots of past question papers from Year 5, so that they can get a feel for the types of questions that get asked. Make a note of the questions that your child is struggling with so that you can go through it at a later stage. If you don't know how to solve a Maths sum please parents, don't be ashamed to ask a friend to help out or look on the internet. It's better to ask for help than to suffer in silence and also make your child suffer.

English

To excel in 11+ English, it's always a good idea to obtain past question papers from the relevant LEA or directly from the relevant Independent schools. It is also possible to make contact with some of the Grammar schools directly to request past question papers. It is important to know the exact format of the exam so that pupils can adequately prepare for that particular format. The English paper usually lasts for between 45 to 60 minutes and it is normally divided into two parts. The questions are designed to test writing skills, vocabulary and the ability to read, understand and assimilate information.

Part A of the 11+ English question paper is usually a comprehension passage with questions. The comprehension is generally based on a passage from classic literature such as Silas Marner by George Eliot. The text can be about 50 to 60 lines long so it is important that pupils can read fast and be able to sieve through information quickly. There will be short questions intended to check that pupils have fully understood what is described in the passage such as characters, feelings and attitudes. Participants will be asked to respond to the passage at greater length e.g. by describing the characters in the story. They will be expected to write clearly, to spell and punctuate reasonably well and to express themselves in grammatically correct English. There will be opportunities for pupils to discuss how or why a writer is using language in a particular way.

Apart from the comprehension questions, the English paper usually comprises other questions on punctuation, synonyms, rewriting sentences correctly and spelling words correctly. If a child is good at reading and creative writing then these are advantageous skills to have for the comprehension section of the exam paper.

General Advice on Excelling in English 11+ Exams

There is a lot of general advice for parents to reiterate to a child when it comes to 11+ writing. Some are outlined below;

- Pupils should avoid using slang and informal language especially colloquial expressions.
- They need to be more alert and focused when speaking, to avoid repetitions and grammatical errors.
- It is important that their writing is neat and well structured.
- For comprehension and creative writing, sentences should be complete and ideas arranged into paragraphs.
- A child should be reminded not to use 'lazy' language that is now commonly used in phone texting.
- Examiners are looking for complete sentences and appropriate use of capital letters and punctuations.

There are various websites some of which are mentioned in this guide that help children with their punctuation and grammar skills. With punctuation, a child will need to focus on knowing when to add capital letters, full stops, apostrophes, question marks, speech marks, exclamation marks, commas and semi-colons. I truly underestimated the importance of having good writing skills and my son had a lot of catching up to do in the last few months leading up to the 11+ exams. I wouldn't want any parent to find themselves in that same situation where these important skills are being perfected at the last minute – literally a few months before the main 11+ exams. It's advantageous to start to prepare a child early and not leave it till the last minute.

To prepare for the 11+, I urge parents to encourage a child to read as many journals, newspaper articles, fiction and non-fiction books as possible. There are a number of websites that have produced long lists of recommended fiction and non- fiction books that can be beneficial. Ensuring a child knows a variety of 11+ vocabulary will make their creative writing stand out. A child should be able to look up the meaning of unusual words from the dictionary and use them in sentences.

A good way for a child to develop their 11+ vocabulary is by parents playing lots of vocabulary building games such as scrabble with them and encouraging them to form new words and check their meanings. I always advised my son to make use of a mixture of similes, metaphors, adjectives, examples of onomatopoeia and alliteration in his speech and writing. In the exam, a child may be required to identify the different parts of speech in a given sentence. Also, I regularly encourage my children to replace the word 'said' with other verbs that imply the same meaning. For instance, my son got used to replacing the verb 'said' with words like 'yelled', 'told', 'bellowed', 'screamed', asked', 'answered', 'whispered' etc. Using such verbs instead of 'said' always make his written work more interesting.

Parent Tip: Encourage your child to summarise what they have read in their own words to ensure they have understood the text.

Creative Writing

11+ entrance exams set by some Grammar and Independent schools require children to complete a Creative Writing exercise as part of the English paper. Pupils are usually given 30 minutes to produce their completed piece of writing. It is paramount that a child's use of grammar and punctuation is very good. The Creative Writing exam will offer candidates the chance to write a story or a description, letter or some equivalent piece of writing. Encourage a child to regularly borrow books from the local library and encourage selection of a wide variety of age-appropriate books that will captivate their interest. Engaging in regular discussions with a child about politics and what is going on in society, will help hone their skills.

In Creative Writing 11+ exams, a child could be given a topic to develop such as 'The Forest', 'Trapped', 'The Dark Shed', 'Describe an elderly relative', 'Describe your best friend' and so on. If a child is given such topics or headings in exam conditions, they will be expected to write a captivating story of at least one and a half to two pages. It is important for pupils to focus on the given topic ensuring that their story stays focused and relevant to the title. They should always write as concisely as possible and should avoid using irrelevant words or jargon. If a child's imaginative skill is not developed through reading, they may struggle to excel in this writing task. They have to be able to think on their feet, plan and get a good story written within 30 minutes.

Parent Tips:

• Ensure your child understands how to use and organise information received through our five senses (sight, hearing, taste, smell and touch) creatively. Also parents should subscribe to children's newspapers that are designed for children aged 7 – 14.

• Please don't force your child to read books that they are not really interested in. It is advisable to take them to a library or a bookstore and allow them to choose a range of books that has caught their attention. Look at it this way...reading something is better than reading nothing.

Verbal Reasoning (VR)

Most Grammar school 11+ exams and Independent school entrance exams include either Verbal Reasoning (VR) or Non Verbal reasoning (NVR) or even both. There are usually about 80 Verbal Reasoning questions and the time allocated to complete the test is usually 50 minutes. Hence, speed is crucial. With the reasoning tests, there are 21 different styles of Verbal Reasoning and these involve topics that require a child to know their spellings, synonyms, antonyms, shapes, meanings of words, sequential codes, finding the opposite of words or the closest in meaning to a word to mention a few. A number of the questions also involve mathematical operations. Some LEAs or schools use at least 15 types of VR questions in their VR exams. Normally, schools do not give out VR past questions.

GL Assessments are the official publishers of the actual 11+ Verbal Reasoning tests that majority of the children will sit. Therefore, it is advisable to purchase some of their resources which are obtainable online and in bookstores.

Some LEAs and Independent schools disclose which types of Verbal Reasoning questions to expect in the exam but some schools don't disclose this information. Therefore, a child will have to be familiar with all the possible types of VR questions that may be asked. It is obvious that a child needs to build a wide range of vocabulary to be able to excel in this subject. Encourage them to use any new words they have learnt in conversations and in their writing. The more practice a child has of the different verbal reasoning styles, the less challenging Verbal Reasoning becomes.

Non-Verbal Reasoning (NVR)

NVR requires that a person understands the reasoning behind shape sequences. The test assesses a child's ability to see patterns and shapes and to point out any errors or inconsistencies such as finding the shape that is the odd one out. A child has to be able to acquire the skills that enable them to see how objects relate to each other. Pupils need to be able to see if a shape or pattern has been rotated to e.g. 45°, 60°, 90°or 180°.

NVR has been described severally over the years as involving the ability to solve complex problems without being limited by language skills. NVR involves the ability to understand and solve problems with visual reasoning. Typical exam papers consist of 60 questions to be completed in 50 minutes. Parents interested in 11+ must start to practice NVR with a child from when they turn age 6. There are a number of age appropriate books at bookstores and online.

What is CEM 11+?

Over the years, some schools have raised concerns about the endemic nature of 11+ coaching or tutoring. Wealthier families have been blamed for hiring tutors to coach their child intensively for 11+. Therefore, a number of LEAs, Independent and Grammar schools have introduced a computer marked CEM 11+ test which assesses and also provides a fair chance for every child regardless of their family background or circumstances. The plan is to make it harder for parents to coach their children to pass the 11+ exam. However, it is still important for a child to revise 11+ subjects which comprise English, Numerical Reasoning and Non-Verbal Reasoning tests. Individual schools determine their pass mark. Candidates are usually given CEM 11+ sample questions upon registration for the exams. I have noticed that there are some unofficial CEM test 11+ practice resources available online and in book stores.

CEM tests are provided by the University of Durham and CEM past question papers have not been made public therefore, there are no complete official sample test papers for sale. However, I have already interviewed a number of children, including my son, who have sat CEM tests and I am duly informed that the tests involve a speed element and are formed of individually timed sections. The CEM tests that my son sat were two sets of 45 minute-long papers administered to all pupils with a break of about 15 to 20 minutes between them. When my son informed me that there were over 100 questions on his CEM 11+ paper, I was shocked as I didn't know what to expect.

Having interviewed a number of pupils who have sat the CEM English and Verbal Reasoning 11+ tests, I have come to a reasonable conclusion that the smartest move for any parent will be to continue to improve on a child's literacy skills through reading. For the CEM tests, speed and fluency are very important skills to have and a good vocabulary will help immensely.

CEM 11+ Maths or Numerical Reasoning

CEM Maths tests a child's mental Maths skills and how good they are at recognising mathematical patterns. It's usually a 30-35 minute non-calculator paper which requires speed. Some of the Maths questions explore problem solving requiring multi-stage processing with a greater reading element.

CEM 11+ English or Verbal Reasoning

CEM 11+ English which is also referred to as Verbal Reasoning includes vocabulary, comprehension, proof reading and literacy exercises. It is essential for a child sitting this exam to have a good vocabulary, reading skills and a clear understanding of synonyms, antonyms, homophones etc. This will also contain a comprehension passage which will require a child to be able to extract information from a passage as required. There will also be a cloze test which is an assessment of a child's comprehension abilities. It includes a portion of text, from which certain words have been removed. Candidates will be required to read an article and decide which words best fits each space.

They will have to insert the missing words according to the context.

I have included a couple of examples below:

- Today, I went to the ___(1)___ and borrowed some books and videos. I knew it was going to snow, but I didn't wear my __(2)___.

- Jayne is a girl of nine. Her home is not____(1)____ from school. She ___(2) ___her bicycle to school daily.

CEM 11+ Non-Verbal Reasoning (NVR)

It's been widely suggested that for NVR, general concepts of rotation, reflection, symmetry, shape, size, position, and shading are important to learn. They are similar to the standard 11+ NVR questions that are widely available.

I hope that you have been able to get an overview of the types of subjects to expect a child to sit for 11+ exams.

Parent Tip: Time management skills are very important for 11+. Make sure that your child practices questions against the clock so they get a feel for what is required of them during the exam.

"Knowledge is power. Information is liberating. Education is the premise of progress, in every society, in every family"

-Kofi Annan

CHAPTER 6
Steps to take before starting the 11+ process

It would be unfair on a child if their parents suddenly decided that they should sit 11+ exams without any prior discussion. It is much better to encourage a child to be part of the decision making process. This will make them feel valued and encourage them to want to work hard. I suggest parents take the following steps:

Speak to the child

It is imperative that parents speak to their child. Parents shouldn't start the process without their child's input. In my case, I took my son to a number of open days held by Grammar and Independent schools when he was in Year 4. From then on, he asked lots of questions about the entry process and made up his mind that he wanted to gain entrance to some of the schools we visited. Therefore, I didn't have to try too hard to convince him of this choice. I was more than happy that it was not a decision that was forced upon him. Had he not made the decision himself, I am certain that I would have tried very hard to convince him to take 11+ because I know he has the ability and I understand the benefits a Grammar school education can afford him.

Parents should do their research

It is crucial that parents thoroughly research the schools they are applying to and the entry criteria. Check the league tables to see the school's performances. Parents should ensure that they are aware of the registration process and the nature of the exams that a child will be sitting. Parents should also be sure that they are happy with the ethos of the schools being considered for their child.

Understand the yearly school report

As parents, it is important to know how to read yearly school reports. Understanding the expected attainment levels of primary school pupils is important. I have endeavoured to explain these in this chapter. This will help parents gauge how well their child is getting on at school and the amount of additional work needed prior to sitting 11+ exams. During my research for this book, I asked a number of parents if they understood their child's report and a lot admitted to me that they didn't understand the coded grades on the report e.g. level 2A,2B etc.

The core stages where schools inform parents of a child's results or levels are at the end of Key Stage 1, which is Year 2 and Key Stage 2 which is at the end of Year 6. Key Stage 1 comprises of Years 1 and 2 and Key Stage 2 comprises of Years 3 to 6. For each subject, at the end of Key Stage 1 and 2, teachers should inform parents of the level that each child has achieved in their school work. The levels act as a gauge for parents to know how well a child is performing in school. It is absolutely vital that parents ask questions if they are unsure of how the levels are achieved.

Various sources have reported the expected attainment levels of pupils in each year group. These are set out below:

Year group and national average age related expectations

Year 1: Level 1b

Year 2: Level 2b

Year 3: Level 2a/ 3c

Year 4: Level 3b

Year 5: Level 3a/4c

Year 6: Level 4b

Some more able children will exceed these expectations, gaining e.g. a Level 3 in Year 2 or a Level 5 or 6 in Year 6. Some children might be struggling with class work and therefore will be performing at a lower standard than is expected of them. Parents who are unsure about how to read results should politely request an explanation from the class teacher.

By summer term of Year 6 a child will be expected to achieve at least a Level 4. Achieving a Level 5 or Level 6 is deemed to be above what is expected and a Level 3 means the child is performing below the expected level for Year 6. I would like to urge parents to please pay attention to the school report.

Recognise a child's academic ability

Parents should identify their child's strengths, talent and personality as well as their weaknesses. Parents need to know if their child is working on a higher or lower level than average. It is important to be equipped with this information in order to support a child with their academic work. Parents should involve themselves in their child's school work and attend all parent evenings to discuss the child's progress in school. If a child is working at a high level in school then it is a good opportunity to start to also prepare them alongside their school work for 11+ exams.

Parents should ensure that they pay attention to the level of work that their child is bringing home from school. Children are grouped into sets in their primary school class rooms. This is done according to ability levels. For parents to make out what level their child is working at, they can for instance check their child's homework spelling list.

How easy or challenging are the words on the spelling list? How challenging is the Maths and English homework given to them by their teacher? The level of work given to a child can indicate if a child is in a lower or higher level set in school. I am sure that some parents are not even aware that this practice is happening in their child's class or school. Schools sometimes use colour codes to mask this practice. For instance, green table might be the brightest kids in class while yellow table sits children with lower ability. In the classroom, the children usually are able to figure out what is going on from the level of work being given out in class.

Some teachers may be reluctant to share this information with parents as some pushy parents might not be happy if their child is in the 'lower ability group'. If a pupil is under-performing, teachers are usually happy to provide regular practise of key skills like reading, writing, spellings, numeracy etc. and are usually willing to work with parents who want to give their child's learning a boost.

Speak to the child's Class Teacher or Head Teacher

Class Teacher

Parents should speak to their child's teacher about what level their child is working at in school. It is a good idea to seek their opinion about a child's suitability for 11+. Be very cautious while taking this step. Some teachers, especially in state primary schools, are not conversant with the 11+ process so parents will have to gauge how much weight to give their input. Parents may not get the encouragement they crave from a child's Class Teacher and this may be discouraging.

I am aware that some teachers find it challenging to identify the capability of some of their pupils and this can happen for a number of reasons. The inability to spot talent can lead to the parents being given incorrect advice regarding suitability for 11+ exams. It's not unusual for pupils to be operating at Level 5 or 6 during complementary tuition but still be held back on Level 4 in their school. In a situation where this has happened, it is possible that pupils have been kept on Level 4 work because the teacher feels that the pupils have not demonstrated the willingness to operate at a higher level.

It is also possible that a teacher is not ready or able to challenge a particular pupil academically. Various studies have shown that a gifted child may become disruptive in class as they are not being adequately challenged academically. A teacher in this situation may place their focus more on the disruptive behaviour rather than the root cause of this behaviour. Instead of labelling this child as being disruptive, it would be more productive if special adjustments could be made both at home and school, to help the child develop their academic and social skills.

Head Teacher

Many Head Teachers are very supportive of the 11+ process. Some Independent schools teach the 11+ curriculum. However, it's important to note that not all Head Teachers support the 11+ process and some schools may not be helpful through this process. Remember! Year 6 is the SATs[9] year for Year 6 pupils in state primary schools and Head Teachers are more concerned about their school's SATs results as this is reflected on the league tables and are also closely monitored by the regulators OFSTED. Some Head Teachers may not be happy that a child may be absent from school for a few days to sit 11+ exams.

Parent Tips:

- A child's Years 4 and 5 school reports are very important. Independent schools usually request these together with the Head Teacher's reference as part of their selection process. Therefore it is important for your child to be focussed and diligent in Year 4 and especially Year 5.

- Some Independent schools hold their 11+ exams on weekdays and it is likely that a child will have to take time off school for these exams. If parents are considering Independent school 11+ exams, it's always a good idea to keep a child's primary school informed of any dates that the child will be absent to sit an 11+ exam. It is standard practice for Independent schools to make a request for references from a child's Head Teacher when parents complete their application form. Therefore, parents are advised to keep their child's Head Teacher in the loop once an application has been made to an Independent school.

- If you have any concerns about your child's progress in school, please speak up and don't suffer in silence. Ask to meet with the class teacher before parent evening. Most teachers like parents who work well with them throughout the term to ensure their child's success.

CHAPTER 7
Essential skills for getting into top Independent schools

Unlike Grammar schools that mainly pick their candidates based on their academic ability, most Independent schools look at other important skills a candidate has. Candidates have to show that they are able to think independently and demonstrate that they have self-management skills amongst many other skills. It is important that parents boost their children's speaking, debating, presentation, research and language skills. I have already mentioned the importance of being able to communicate properly. Please find outlined below a few skills that could help pupils obtain generous offers of scholarship at an Independent school.

Learn a musical instrument
Learning an instrument is like learning a new language and it can be very challenging. There are a number of reasons why it is beneficial for a child to learn an instrument. It has been widely suggested by scientists that children that know how to play an instrument perform better in their academic work

than those who do not have any musical skill.

If parents are considering applying to Independent schools and increasing their child's chances of obtaining a good scholarship, it is advisable that the child starts to learn a musical instrument from when they are in reception Year or in Year 1 of Primary School (around 4-6 years old). A number of Independent schools award between 50% to 100% of the school fees as scholarships to children that have attained a minimum of Grade 4 or 5 in relevant music exams. The higher the exam grades obtained in a musical instrument, the better the opportunity it presents the child when it is time to apply for music scholarships. Parents should hire a brilliant tutor who teaches their child's preferred instrument. The truth is that if parents don't start their child at a very early age on the graded exams in a musical instrument; there is no way the child can reach a Grade 4 or 5 standard in music by the age of 10 or 11.

Music skills will help a child's brain develop. There are a number of research studies that have been carried out which support this notion. Learning a musical instrument is not an easy skill and each child is different and learns at a different pace. For music exams in Violin for instance, there is usually the prep test then Grade 1 to Grade 8 totalling 9 different graded exams. On average, it takes between 6-12 months or even longer depending on the child and tutor, to thoroughly prepare for one graded music exam. So imagine the challenge ahead. A child needs to practice on their musical instrument daily so they can thoroughly gain the skills required to excel in their graded exams.

I personally know a 10 year old girl who had already attained a Grade 8 in her violin accredited exams before she sat the 11+. As a result of her rare musical achievement, every Independent school to which she had applied was literally begging her to join with 100% scholarships. Imagine such good fortune! She was spoilt for choice. Fantastic!

Get involved in sporting activities

A good number of Independent schools award scholarships to children who can prove that they are of exceptional standard in at least one of the major sports played at the school. Some of the popular sports at Independent schools are: swimming, athletics, tennis, rugby, cricket and football. It is beneficial if a child is involved in sports competitively so they can stand out amongst the crowd. It would be good to try to juggle at least one or two sporting activities into their already packed schedule. Independent schools want to see evidence that a child has represented their present school in local competitions, competed at county level, national level or better still, international sporting competitions. The whole process is very competitive; therefore schools are looking for the 'Crème de la crème'.

Get involved in Drama

If a child has a flair for Drama, parents should encourage and nurture this skill. Parents should ensure that they find the child a qualified Drama teacher or a good Drama school to attend. Drama promotes self-confidence as well as better public speaking skills in children. Independent schools award scholarships to children who show exceptional ability in this subject. If a child is applying for a Drama scholarship, the child will be interviewed and asked to audition for senior staff.

The child will be expected to have a positive attitude towards Drama as well as good physical and vocal skills. They will be expected to participate fully in school productions and to act as positive role models in behaviour and commitment. It is usually a condition of the award that they continue to do so.

Get involved in Art

When it comes to Art, a number of Independent schools will award scholarships to a child who display creativity and flair and who is committed to participating in Art and pursuing Art throughout their school life and beyond. Schools usually request that a child interested in applying for an 11+ scholarship submits a portfolio of no more than six pieces of recent work and a sketchbook which displays evidence of independent study and a desire to create Art, rather than a need for a scholarship portfolio.

A typical[10] 11+ timetable for admission to an Independent school

Dates	11+ Event
March - October 2013	Application process
October 2013	Application process ends
Late November 2013	Child (applicant) sits test in Maths, English, Verbal and/or Non-Verbal Reasoning.
Jan - March 2014	Interview and Oral English test
Jan - March 2014	Talent award day – schools decide who is awarded scholarships
Jan – March 2014	Preferred school requests reference from applicant's school
March 2014	School expects parents to confirm if accepting offers made to their child and some schools may request an acceptance fee or advance payment of first term's school fees

Parent Tip: A flair for Drama will help your child make creative choices and help them have the ability to think up new ideas and have an imaginative mind.

CHAPTER 8
Parental commitments and sacrifices before and during the 11+ process

Parents make a lot of commitments towards the 11+ process in a quest for their child to attend schools that are rated top in the UK and in the world. So many families from countries in Asia, Africa and Europe for instance place a very high value on British education and a record number of families now ensure that their children also sit the 11+ entrance exams so that they can attend top UK Independent schools. This has also made the competition for spaces fiercer. Below are some examples of the level of commitment parents will make during the 11+ process.

Financial Commitment

There is a lot of financial commitment involved in the process. This includes the cost of 11+ tutoring and revision materials.

Some parents choose to send their children to Independent junior schools from the age of four. This is an expensive option for many as school fees usually start from about £2,000 per term. These schools have a smaller number of children per class and they are not required to follow the national curriculum. As a result, the schools are able to teach 11+ syllabuses and freely coach their pupils for the 11+ exams. The other reasons that parents generally give for taking this step are that Private schools raise children that are more confident, driven and have access to a greater range of extra-curricular activities.

The unspoken reason why some parents send their children to such schools is because they believe that mixing with other financially capable families builds contacts and improves their children's chances of networking with people of similar affluent background. Obviously pupils that attend state Primary schools are less privileged when it comes to 11+ preparations. They have to follow the national curriculum in school which does not consist of any 11+ work. Therefore, any extra tutoring or coaching would have to take place after school and at a very high cost to their parents.

Moving House

Yearly, a good number of children are missing out on Grammar school places due to the fact that they do not reside in the catchment area of their chosen Grammar schools. I am aware of a number of families that have taken the bold step of moving closer to the schools they would like their child to attend. It is therefore advisable for parents to start considering suitable schools early and start searching for nearby homes early – possibly between two to three years before a child is even ready to sit their 11+. Parents need to remember one thing; there are many families out there that are also thinking of doing the same thing. So, it is advisable to start the process early.

Tutoring Costs

Most 11+ tutors charge about £25-£50 an hour. Usually the tutors inform parents that as well as the tutoring, this amount also covers the lesson materials, planning, tutor's travel costs, photocopying etc.

Tutoring costs: Music lessons, Drama classes and Art classes

For parents who are considering Independent school education for their child, it was mentioned earlier that it is important that a child participates actively in at least one of the following extra curricular activities: Sports, Music, Art or Drama. Parents usually spend a fortune on these activities as they are deemed necessary for the admissions process.

Transportation costs

Parents usually have to bear the transportation costs involved in shuttling children to and from tutoring sessions, sporting activities, open days etc.

Non-refundable registration fees

Some Grammar schools and Independent schools charge non-refundable registration fees during the application stage. This amount can range from between £50 - £300. If a child does not sit the test set by the schools on the scheduled exam date, then the child's parents may have to forfeit the fees already paid.

Taking time off from work

Some parents take extensive time off work to self-tutor their children and revise with them. Parents will also need time off work to shuttle their child to exam venues as well.

Forfeiting a good holiday

The whole family may have to forfeit their holidays in the run up to 11+ exams in order to allow a child to focus and continue with their revision. It is a fact that parents feel guilty about going on holiday near 11+ exams knowing that other children are revising. Competition is fierce!

Hidden costs of attending Grammar and Independent Schools

There are some hidden costs that no one tells parents about unless they ask the questions. Usually parents start to find out about these extra costs after a child has passed their 11+ exams for entrance either to a Grammar school or an Independent school. For example the cost of the school uniform which is usually sourced from special outfitters can be as high as £1000. This will cover the cost of the school blazer, smart trousers, school rugby shirts, mouth guard, school shoes, rugby boots, football boots, school tie, tail suits, football kit to name a few. Don't forget that a child may need to get more than one set of uniforms.

Also parents may want to pay the cost of music tuition if they want their child to continue learning a musical instrument in school. The cost of taking music lessons in school starts from about £140 per term. There is also the cost of hiring or purchasing a musical instrument which is usually around £30-£50 per term depending on the instrument.

Furthermore, parents will need to consider transportation costs when making a decision about the choice of school. Some children attend schools in a different County to where they live and as a result, some parents pay up to £800 per term on transportation costs depending on the distance of the home to school. In some instances, parents group together to hire a coach service to ferry their children to and from school. There is usually a collection and drop off point with agreed timings. Parents will have to arrange to have their children met at the drop-off point. Be prepared for other associated costs for school trips abroad, field trips, pocket money and so on.

"Education begins at home and I applaud the parents who recognise that they – not someone else – must take responsibility to assure that their children are well educated".

-Ernest Istook

CHAPTER 9
Rising above 11+ secrecy and How to avoid distractions during 11+ revision

Rising above 11+ secrecy

The 11+ process is the best kept secret amongst parents. A number of parents and schools either refuse to talk about it openly or refuse to share information with other parents about topics such as resources available and tutoring for 11+. Some parents keep quiet about really good tutors. Some others even hide the resource materials that their child is using when visitors come round. Yes! The secrecy is that bad.

I later discovered through speaking to lots of parents and 11+ candidates that some parents even use up to five different tutors to coach their child for this process. Please don't be so surprised because it's happening.

Here is one parent's comment when she was asked about her child's tutor. She actually said "I can't give you my child's tutor's details as I don't want her to take on more children. If she takes on more children, she will have less time for my child". This is the type of self-centred behaviour on display by some parents during this 11+ process. Some parents even go to the extent of being deceitful and claiming that their children aren't taking the 11+ exams in an attempt to dissuade others from the 11+ route. Some others mislead fellow parents by convincing them that their child is not receiving any tuition or help at all as their child is a just a whiz kid. Please be weary of parents that tell you such baloney as it is more likely there's something they are not telling you.

It's disheartening when I see the level of ignorance amongst a lot of parents when it comes to sharing information about the 11+ process. I would like to encourage parents to search online for useful resources and books that can provide sufficient information on the 11+ process. Parents should avoid secrecy as it only fosters ignorance.

 **Parent Tip:** The best way to find out information about the whole 11+ process is to speak to parents whose children have already been through the process. It is highly unlikely that they will withhold information from you or mislead you as you are not seen as a threat to their child's success if their child hopefully has already secured a place in their preferred Grammar or Independent school.

How to avoid distractions during 11+ revision
To help a child stay focused during the 11+ process, parents should endeavour to set up a study area that is quiet and conducive in their home.

Distractions and interruptions are time wasters and parents must help their child manage their time more effectively and wisely while studying for 11+ exams. Nearer my son's 11+ exams, we grudgingly suspended his attendance at Saturday football, Scouts and many sleepover offers. He was gutted and unhappy about this decision but as parents we made him understand why this was happening. He later understood that we were not being cruel towards him. Some of these events clashed with his 11+ tutoring slot. I made him realise that the focus and determination of an Olympic winning athlete is required to win the 11+ race. Team work between the child and parents is crucial too. A child accomplishing the 4-6 hours revision time daily is very feasible but challenging. With all of today's technology and distractions it is hard to study at times.

It is essential that parents and their children avoid unnecessary distractions like TV blaring, emails waiting to be read, phones ringing, text messages beeping and so on. These could all cause poor study habits. Parents need to ensure that their child isn't distracted by mobile phones and social networking websites and should turn off anything that can cause a disturbance to a child until they have finished their revision. Parents should try and spend most of their free time helping their child with their 11+ revision and having valuable discussions with them. There are a number of distractions that can make even parents lose track or lose interest in successfully pursuing the 11+ route. There are pressures from work and some parents don't feel they have enough time to dedicate to the process. There are other social, avoidable distractions such as parents being pre-occupied with social networking websites, parents spending long hours at work and many other factors.

 **Parent Tip:** Please ensure that your child is not encouraged to own a phone that gives them the freedom to chat with friends uncontrollably. I know of 10 Year olds who are already addicted to such phones. In the months leading up to 11+ parents should guard against this.

"All I have learned, I learned from books"

-Abraham Lincoln

"When you know better you do better."

-Maya Angelou

CHAPTER 10

What preparation is required for the exam?

Let me put things into perspective, the reality is that for every one space available at Grammar and Independent schools, it's estimated that there are about 10-12 applicants. Someone I know even commented that "The preparation for the 11+ is more challenging than preparing for a job interview with an investment bank."

Preparation needed for 11+ will vary between each child and will also depend on the type of primary or preparatory school a child is currently attending. I mentioned earlier that some Independent preparatory schools prepare their pupils for 11+ from a young age. Therefore, a child who has attended a state primary school will probably require more intensive preparation for 11+ than one that has attended an Independent school from the age of four.

The following are important steps for parents and their child to take in preparation for the exams:

Practice time management techniques

The truth is that 11+ is one of the most challenging and competitive exams that a child will ever take and they have just one opportunity to sit and pass the exam. It is important for a child to learn to manage their time effectively in an exam of any length and they have to learn to remain calm and focussed during the exams while working both accurately and speedily through the papers.

Build their vocabulary and comprehension skills

I would say that the preparation for 11+ begins from when a child is still a baby. What do I mean by this? Well, parents need to start nurturing their child from when they are really young, in a way that would prepare them for the 11+ route. For instance, parents can start building a child's vocabulary from an early age by talking to them and not just leaving them sitting before the television for long hours. It's beneficial to start reading to a child long before they even start to understand the meaning of words. This behaviour gives them an advantage in expanding their language skills. It would also encourage such children to develop a life-long love of reading.

Ideally, the best time to start intensive preparation with a child for the 11+ exams is when they reach Year 4. They will have enough time to cover a lot of work on the 11+ curriculum and get familiarised with the type of questions that may be asked. It is advisable that parents frequently listen to their child read and engage in meaningful dialogue with them. This will help increase the confidence and creativity in their speech and their writing skills. Furthermore, it is important for parents to focus on a child's comprehension skills to ensure that their child has the ability to think about, understand and interpret what they have read and connect this to the information they already know. These pointers will definitely help immensely in tackling entrance exams.

Set limits on TV time

I don't have to delve into the research that many experts have already carried out on the adverse effects of unlimited television viewing and children engaging in unchecked and unreasonable use of computer games. Watching too much TV damages a child's creativity, intelligence and other physical skills. Therefore, part of the preparation is to reduce the amount of television and computer games playing that a child is exposed to. Parents will realise that this will help their concentration skills. Ideally, TV is something that should be limited and not placed in a child's bedroom to help them fall asleep. If it's in the bedroom, the parents can start to lose control over what their child is watching and the amount of time spent on it.

Parent Tip: Assessment by an 11+ tutor

It is advisable for parents to ensure that before finalising a tutor place for their child, they arrange for an 11+ tutor to assess their child in English, Maths, VR and NVR and give them a comprehensive written report on their child's performance including the marked test papers. The assessment will test a child's ability, potential and their willingness to learn. The benefit of this step is two-fold. Firstly, the parents are able to assess the tutor and have an opportunity to discuss any concerns they may have. Secondly, the tutor will have the opportunity to know some of the child's weaknesses and strengths. Guess what parents! Some tutors charge between £35 and £50 for this assessment.

Tutoring

It is almost unfeasible to find any child who has not had one form of tutoring during this 11+ process. Don't be deceived by some parents that may inform you that their child was never tutored. Really! Their child must have the brain of Albert Einstein. Good tutors will be able to give a child important tips and techniques to excelling in 11+ and that's why a lot of parents go for this option. Great tutors are able to evaluate their student's performance and work on any weaknesses discovered. They will also have the ability to use homework to gauge a child's understanding of topics. I know of a number of parents who hired tutors for their children from age 4. I am not suggesting that parents start tutoring their children from this young age; I am just keeping parents informed of the realities of the 11+ process. Parents are becoming increasingly aware of the amount of hard work involved in getting through the 11+ syllabus and the amount of competition out there. In my opinion, at the tender ages of between 4-7 years, learning should not be as intense because these young ones still have a few years before sitting the 11+. In fact, young children should enjoy learning and not even realise that the tasks they are being given are preparing them for the 11+.

A survey by website elevenplusexams.co.uk which provides a lot of resources on 11+, reported that more than six out of ten parents believed that 11+ tutoring increased their child's opportunity of passing the 11+ exams. It is so important that parents complement whatever involvement an external tutor has with their child. As a parent, I find that there is always the temptation to get really worked up and deflated if a child is not showing interest or is not reaching the level of understanding that is expected of them. When my son was revising for the 11+, I had a number of frustrating moments only because I thought that he wasn't pulling his weight.

It's always important for parents to establish the topics that their child is struggling with so that they can find the simplest method of explaining these topics to them. Due to the fact that a number of Independent primary schools assist with preparing their pupils for 11+, there is always the temptation for parents to become laid back and feel that they don't have to do any additional work with their child. This is a serious misconception. It is vital that parents check that the homework given to their child by the tutor is tackled by the child. The homework reinforces all the learning and gives a confidence boost to the child.

Parents have to assess their child to know the type of tutoring that would best work for them. I know that due to the rising cost of 11+ tutoring, a number of parents have resorted to self-tutoring to save costs. It could get really challenging for parents to self-tutor especially if the nature of their employment demands that they work really long hours and weekends. In this instance, it will be advisable to get a private tutor to coach the child through the process; obviously this comes at a cost. Some private tutoring can be on a one to one basis or a child could be in a group with other children. My advice is that parents should observe carefully to ensure that their child is benefitting from whichever option is chosen.

In my opinion, I would recommend that parents try and put their child in a small tuition group rather than in a large group where the child may be distracted. Recommendations from friends, family or previous 11+ candidates are usually the best and simplest way to find a good tutor.

Identify the exam format and prepare adequately
The prospectus and the school's website should give parents information about what the school's 11+ comprises. This will give parents the opportunity to provide adequate support to their child and equip them with the right skills needed to excel in the relevant subjects.

Prepare a revision timetable

It is advisable for parents to sit with their child and prepare a timetable that would contain the set times for them to revise for each 11+ subject. It is important for parents to dedicate time towards revising with their child. Parents should set up a routine for their child and choose realistic times. Ensure that the child has not got other activities booked. Parents should avoid all distractions and ensure they give room for some flexibility.

 **Parent Tip:** Prior to Year 5, it is important that parents spend at least three hours a week revising with their child in subjects such as English, Maths, Creative Writing and just generally brushing up on their school work. This will benefit their child in the long run.

Daily revision and parental involvement

From school Year 5, children who are getting ready for the 11+, need to achieve at least 4-6 hours of revision work every day. This level of revision is intense. It is important to ensure that a child understands and enjoys the basics of Maths such as their times tables. It is imperative that they practice their Maths skills regularly. During my research, I discovered that a number of 11+ candidates wake up as early as 6am and they get through one or more revision practice papers before going to school. Their revision also continues when they return from school. The key to excelling is for a child to work through a lot of practice papers in a structured way with a tutor who is able to give them guidance, techniques and plenty of tips. I hope this book gives parents some exposure into the secrets that some 11+ parents will not reveal.

Watch the time

Parents should ensure that their child watch the time whenever they are given any practice test papers. A child has to progressively develop the discipline of time management in timed exam conditions.

Parents! Pay attention

Review a child's 11+ revision tasks regularly to see which topics or questions they are struggling with the most. For instance, if parents notice a particular area of Maths, Verbal Reasoning, Non-verbal Reasoning or English a child is struggling with then it is advisable that parents go over these areas in detail. Parents should look online and print off questions pertaining to that topic and ensure that they go through the topic thoroughly with the child or ask their 11+ tutor to help out.

Past question papers

If parents can get their hands on past question papers from the relevant schools to which they have applied, they should invest some money in these. Some schools or LEAs charge a fee for their past question papers. A lot of Independent schools especially, give copies of Maths and English past papers once parents have completed the registration process.

Revision resources

There are thousands of materials in bookstores all professing to be the 'best' for 11+ revisions. These materials cover the main 11+ subjects. I found that there were so many resources that anyone would get confused. I did a lot of impulse buying. You know what? I ended up not even opening some of the revision packs and have given some away and saved some for my younger children. My advice is that parents should be careful of which resources they purchase. There are many ways to practise for entrance tests. There are so many free tests online.   The best way forward is to ask parents who have been through the process to share their experiences. They will be able to provide information about what resources worked well for their child and the reasons why. Some of the materials published on some 11+ websites are not free to access and parents may be required to register for a fee.

It is advisable to use age appropriate books widely sold in bookstores to encourage a child to practice the 11+ subjects. I normally start with age appropriate resources from age 5-6 years. I then go over my children's work and make the necessary corrections. One of the mistakes that some parents make is that they give work to their child and then fail to check if the child understood the task or even completed the task. Encourage a child to continue to work through these age appropriate books until the child sits all their exams.

Playing educational games

Prior to a child reaching Year 5, it is advisable to engage their minds and increase their concentration skills by allowing them to for example, play a game of chess regularly and to play word games such as crosswords and scrabble to help develop their vocabulary. These games and many other useful games can be played online.

Attend 11+ mock tests

The main purpose of mock tests is to provide a candidate with the chance to experience what it's like to sit 11+ exams under the same conditions as will apply in their real entrance exams. Mock exams usually help alleviate any fears or nerves and helps children familiarise themselves with the new process. There are written mock tests in Verbal Reasoning, Non-Verbal Reasoning, English and Maths, which simulates real exam conditions. Results will be ranked to show how a child performed compared to other children.

Kindle device or any e-reader

Download a lot of fiction and non-fiction books to a kindle device or any other e-reader. There are a number of suggested reading lists for ages 8-11 online. Please refrain from downloading games on the device as children might show more interest in playing these games than in reading any books you have downloaded.

Parent Tips:

- Give your child lots of praise if they have done well in the revision tasks given to them. Also, regularly acknowledge their hard work and dedication but don't dwell too much on how smart you think they are. Boost their performance with encouraging words even if they have not impressed you with their performance on test papers. I realised that making threats only fell on deaf ears so it's not worth going down that route.

- Regularly give your child a treat during their revision especially when you have promised them one. Give your child lots of hugs during the 11+ process. It's such a stressful time for them and they need to be pampered and encouraged.

- Encourage your child to read to you as reading will help their vocabulary a lot.

"In order to succeed, your desire for success should be greater than your fear of failure"-

-Bill Cosby

CHAPTER 11
When does 11+ take place?

Truly, the best advice is for parents to make contact directly with their preferred schools to find out this piece of information. The dates of selection tests to Grammar schools vary from LEA to LEA, but generally speaking most state Grammar schools make 11+ candidates sit their exams in the September of when a child is in Year 6. Although some Independent schools start to examine candidates from when they are still in Year 5, actually most Independent schools examine 11+ candidates between September and March when they are in Year 6. My son sat one of his exams on the 3rd January, at the start of spring term of Year 6. So awkward! That year, Christmas wasn't so much fun for him. There was an absolute ban on chocolates as I didn't want him munching on anything that would affect his concentration skills and I also wanted to reduce the risk of him falling ill.

LEAs will usually publicise information about exam dates on their website. Parents can also check for information on their preferred school's website. For the application process to Grammar schools, it is imperative that parents start enquiring about the registration process and the exam timetable from the September of when their child is in Year 5 or earlier. Please remember that most registration processes especially for Grammar schools take place around spring/summer term of when a child is in Year 5.

Parents should contact Independent schools in plenty of time to confirm their registration process and when their 11+ entrance exams will be held. Knowing these exam dates will also help parents plan the dates to attend open mornings and open evenings.

I have added a table in this chapter to show a chronology of typical events that normally take place in the months leading up to the 11+ exams and the processes leading up to the admissions stage. It is important to make a note of exam dates in a diary to avoid forgetting about the dates and preventing double-bookings especially if a child is sitting a number of exams for different schools. It is important for parents to keep tabs on dates so they don't miss the deadlines for the application process. Parents have to also ensure that they obtain and complete the necessary registration forms within any set deadlines. I am aware of the fact that some Independent schools will not offer bursaries or scholarships if applicants miss the set deadlines for the submission of bursary or scholarship applications.

Late Registration for 11+ exams

Late registration for Grammar school 11+ exams means that if a child achieves the qualifying pass mark, they will not be offered a Grammar school place on the National Offer Day[11] which is usually in the first week of March (spring term) of when 11+ candidates are in Year 6. The child will be put on the waiting lists for schools that they have achieved the qualifying score and applied to. Therefore parents should ensure that they complete the registration process early.

Exam day and exam venue

Usually Grammar school 11+ exams take place in one day. The exam day will consist of timed sessions in the morning and afternoon. 11+ candidates will normally take the exams at their own primary school and this is the case in Kent LEA. Children who attend primary schools outside a particular LEA area, will normally take the 11+ exam at a separate exam venue and a different exam date is usually set for such candidates.

With Independent school exams, candidates usually sit their 11+ exams at the preferred schools to which they have directly applied. The admission process could take between 1 to 3 days and 11+ candidates have to get through a number of obstacles in order to be successful. In my experience, some Independent schools have 'talent award' test days whereby children who have applied for scholarships in Art, Music, Drama or Sport will be able to show case their talents so that scholarships can be awarded to those that perform exceptionally well.

As part of the assessment process, some Independent schools invite 11+ applicants over for residential assessments in their boarding facility. Again, this is a form of interview process designed to test a child's independence and leadership qualities and ability to cope under pressure, ability to use their initiative, communication skills, teamwork etc. It is a good idea for parents to teach their child, interview techniques and skills in case they are confronted with this situation.

A Typical chronology of 11+ events - To be used only as a guide[1]

June/July 2013	Consortium[1] Schools Open Days/Evenings
3rd June 2013	Online registration begins for consortium 11+ exams for September 2014 entry
6th September 2013	Deadline to register online or by post for consortium 11+ exams
11th September 2013	Candidate reference number and test centre information posted to candidates
21st September 2013	11+ exam day
30th September 2013	Alternative test day for religious, illness or exceptional circumstances only
15th October 2013	11+ results received by candidates
31st October 2013	Parents submit Common Application Form (CAF) to the LEA
3rd March 2014	National offer date – LEA to send out secondary school offers to parents

Parent Tips

- Some LEAs like Kent County Council usually hold 11+ mock exams a week before the main exams. All registered candidates are invited to attend but it's not compulsory.

- The registration process for some Independent schools' 11+ take place months earlier when a child is still in Year 5. Apply early and don't leave it till the last minute.

---

1   This table is a guide only. It lists the important dates highlighted by the Consortium of Selective Schools Essex (CSSE). Please note that these dates change annually therefore parents have to check for new dates on the relevant LEA or consortium's website.

CHAPTER 12

Where can parents obtain information about good secondary schools?

Apart from relying on information obtained from friends and associates, there are a number of websites that offer free information about Grammar and Independent schools. LEAs' websites usually publish information about all the Grammar, Independent and Comprehensive schools in their local area. Although parents are able to search online for necessary information, I have outlined other reputable sources where information can be obtained.

Open Mornings and Open Evenings

This is a parent's chance to be a nosey parker and become overly inquisitive. It is an excellent opportunity to find out more about the school and meet their staff and pupils. Even though parents would have had a lot of lovely, colourful, glossy prospectuses come through the post; there is absolutely nothing that can beat paying the school a visit with the child. Parents will be able to speak to the teachers, current pupils and other parents and will have the opportunity to ask "a buffet of questions" as my son put it. Parents will be able to check out boarding facilities if this option is being considered for their child and can enquire about vital topics such as the school's academic performance, pastoral care, bursaries, scholarships, ground rules and so on. Ultimately, parents will be able to capture the culture of the school and ascertain whether they feel their child will be able to fit in and adapt to the culture of the school. Parents are able to check the standards of the school's facilities and a number of extra-curricular events that have been displayed on the school notice boards.

OFSTED Reports

OFSTED is an independent and an impartial body which inspects and regulates UK services that care for children and young people, and those providing education and skills for learners of all ages. In the UK, OFSTED carry out hundreds of inspections and regulatory visits throughout England and publishes its findings on its website. Parents can access OFSTED reports online for the latest assessment of any UK secondary school. It is important that parents read the report for the school of their choice. After an inspection, OFSTED inspectors produce a report that outlines the effectiveness of the inspected school. The report also outlines any recommendations for improvement.

Criticising Comprehensive schools, OFSTED recently released a statement which stated that "Two-thirds of pupils, some 65,000 who achieved Level 5 in Primary school Maths and English tests failed to get A* or an A in both subjects at GCSE" – **OFSTED** 13 June 2013.

School attainment tables or performance tables

These are also commonly known as league tables. The Performance table of schools is a list which compares schools. It ranks them in order of ability or achievement and this set of tables informs the public about the achievements of children in schools throughout England. It is worthwhile for parents to check the performance table of schools in the UK and not to just choose the school next door to their home. It gives a good indication of performing and non-performing schools. Some schools are performing so badly that they should not even be considered an option.

Performance table usually shows the GCSE and A'level ranking of schools. For instance, it reveals how many schools met the threshold of pupils achieving five GCSEs at grade A*-C. It is common to find parents who don't have any knowledge of the fact that such information exists. Some parents do not know the usefulness of these tables until it is explained to them. I found that a number of parents are not bothered about checking the performance table. I am not so naive as to be unaware that some parents actually don't care about the performance table; but I would suggest that they should be used as a guide to help parents choose the best school for their child.

The Good Schools Guide

The Good Schools Guide provides information on Comprehensive, Grammar and Independent schools. It gives an idea of the kind of child a particular school would suit. It provides answers to a lot of questions that parents would like to know about a school such as their academic strengths and location of school. It also gives great tips to parents on a variety of useful topics. This guide is available to purchase from bookshops or online.

How do parents know which Grammar or Independent school will be suitable for their child?

It's a great question which is usually on a lot of parents' minds. Apart from the points mentioned in the preceding paragraphs, it is important that parents give utmost priority to their child's personal needs and preference. Ideally, the choice of school should suit their child's interests, talents and personality.

Also, I would strongly advise parents to consider the candid opinions of students already attending the preferred schools. Their perspective will be invaluable as they are likely to share more information than what any of the Class Teachers or Head Teacher would divulge. More important than academic achievements is whether the school has clear core values and beliefs. It is also important to find out if the pupils already attending the school are positive about their experience of the school. Also, it is likely that a school's website might shed some light on the values of the school so I would urge parents to trawl through their preferred school's website for information.

It is also important to become familiar with the admissions criteria of all the preferred school choices. Realistically, there are some Grammar schools that will not consider a child who does not live in their catchment area. Therefore, it is important for parents to consider the distance between the school and their house before making their decision. My advice is for parents to look at realistic options rather than waste time hoping their child will gain admission to such schools. If parents are not prepared to move home then please consider ruling out these options. Competition is so fierce that there is only a small chance of a candidate living outside of the catchment area gaining admission to such schools.

Parents need to assess their child to find out if the qualities they have will help them to excel and thrive in the school environment being considered. Even siblings have different qualities and each child therefore needs a school that will be suitable for them. A school that is ideal for child A might not be the best option for child B. Each child is different and has different abilities and skills sets.

Parents know their child's abilities therefore they should look for schools that have programmes designed to enhance these. For instance, if a child is good in music, parents must ensure that the school can continue to nurture these skills. If a child loves particular sports, check that the school has a team that the child can join. Attending open days and open evenings might help alleviate any fears a child or their parents may have and answer any burning questions.

Parent Tips:

- Although it's always good to talk to other parents who are better informed than you, please proceed with caution. Ask for their opinion on schools and also DO YOUR OWN RESEARCH! Don't rely solely on information given to you by others. Every child is different and it's important that you look out for your child's individual needs before choosing a school.

- As Parents, you will eventually just have to follow your instincts!

"We have an obligation and a responsibility to be investing in our students and our schools. We must make sure that people who have the grades, the desire and the will but not the money, can still get the best education possible"

-President Barack Obama

CHAPTER 13
How to prepare for schools admissions process

After going through the 11+ exams, the next stage is for parents to prepare for the admissions process. There are different elements to this stage. Usually LEAs, Grammar and Independent schools provide the necessary information to parents. The admissions process start even before the 11+ exams are taken so it's essential for parents to keep abreast of information. I will provide answers below to the frequently asked questions relevant to this process.

When is the deadline for applying to the LEA?

The new Schools 2012 Admissions code promotes an admissions system that allows all state school places to be allocated and offered in a fair way. This code took effect for admissions for entry in September 2013. It stipulates that schools must take all reasonable steps to inform parents of the outcome of 11+ tests, before the closing deadline for applications to the LEA due on October 31st of the year an applicant is in Year 6. The application to the LEA is done by parents completing a Common Application Form (CAF). Information about the CAF is provided in the next paragraph.

What is the Common Application Form (CAF)?

The Local Authority is required by law to co-ordinate admissions to Year 7 at all secondary schools except Independent schools in the borough. The CAF is the form that each Local Authority must provide parents residing in that particular borough so that they can express their school preferences. The LEA gives this form to all parents whose children are transitioning to secondary school.

The CAF is usually given to all parents in the spring or summer term of when their child is in Year 5. This form is used by parents to state their child's secondary school preferences, usually six choices, in order of priority. If a child has passed the 11+, the parents will be required to list their preferred Grammar schools on the CAF form as well as any Comprehensive schools under consideration.

The CAF should not be used to list any Independent schools parents are considering for their child; parents must apply directly to those Independent schools. For a child's secondary school application to be considered valid, the CAF can either be completed online or by parents completing a paper version. The CAF must be submitted online to the LEA's admissions website or parents must hand in the form at their child's primary school. The school will then be responsible for returning the completed CAF to the LEA before the deadline.

Parents must complete the CAF for the LEA in which they reside at the date of the application. The home Local Authority is usually regarded as the one where parents pay their Council Tax bill. The schools that parents choose to list on the CAF can be located anywhere in the UK but must be part of the co-ordinated admissions system. Parents are able to check if a school is part of the co-ordinated admissions system on their LEA's website. Once 11+ results are received and a child has obtained the qualifying marks in their 11+ exams, it is advisable for parents to list all the preferred Grammar schools above any other school preference.

For Year 7 admissions, the deadline for submission of the CAF to the LEA is usually the 31st October of when a child is in Year 6. An advantage of this is that the child would have received their 11+ results before 31st October and parents would have had the opportunity to whittle down a list of the schools they would be happy for their child to attend. If all six schools that they have listed are in a position to offer the child a place in accordance with their published admissions criteria, then the system will automatically seek the highest preference and this is what the child will be allocated. It is advisable that when completing the CAF, parents should always put the schools in the real order of preference.

What is the Supplementary Information Form (SIF)?

Some Grammar and Comprehensive schools might require parents to complete a SIF as well as add them on the list of school preferences on the CAF. If parents are applying for a school that requires a SIF, the SIF must be obtained directly from the school or the school's website, completed and returned directly to the school within the stated deadline. In some instances, the deadline for the return of SIF directly to the relevant school can be before the CAF submission deadline.

Not all Grammar schools or Comprehensive schools require parents to complete a SIF. Some schools use the SIF to determine how well a child meets the school's admissions criteria. A number of Grammar schools, Comprehensive, Faith and oversubscribed schools have SIFs. SIF requests additional details which assist schools in applying their admissions criteria. If the SIF and CAF are not completed within the stipulated deadlines, the schools often do not have waiting lists and may not consider a child's application. It is crucial not to miss application deadlines.

Parent Tips:

• Applying for only one school and listing it six times on the CAF will definitely not increase any child's chances of being offered a place at that particular school. Therefore, choose wisely!

• You can obtain SIF directly from your preferred school if the school requires one to be completed. Be mindful of Supplementary Information Forms (SIF) submission deadlines.

• Don't panic! Parents will receive adequate information about CAF closing dates from their child's primary school and from their LEA.

CHAPTER 14
Financial Assistance - Applying For Scholarship, Bursary & Educational Grants

Apart from parents remortgaging their homes, using their savings or taking out loans to pay for their child's school fees, there are other sources of financial assistance available to students. For instance, bursaries, grants and scholarships can give a lot of children from all walks of life access to the best education without them having to pay the full cost of it. As I mentioned earlier, due to the fact that Independent schools' fees are out of reach for a number of families, bursaries and scholarships are usually awarded to help families with the school fees. Almost all Independent schools offer some measure of financial support. Educational grants are also available in some cases.

Scholarship

A scholarship is a means of financial assistance provided by another body or institution so that a child can pursue a line of education that may not be accessible or affordable to them under normal circumstances. Scholarships are usually awarded on merit to pupils that perform exceptionally well in entrance exams or tests.

As previously mentioned, Independent schools offer scholarships to children that are talented in Music, Sports, Art and Drama. Independent schools like to see exceptional talent. For instance, if a child is in the National sports team, Olympic team or playing for their local County then this will make that child really stand out during the scholarship process. Even though a child may be very intelligent, they may still not be offered a scholarship. Scholarships are not means tested and are granted on a limited number of places per year. Their values vary from school to school and from child to child. They can go from a 10% reduction in school fees up to 100%. A child granted 100% scholarship will not have to pay any school fees. In addition to this, some candidates may not even have to pay towards any school trips and some other school expenses.

It is more prevalent now that a scholarship carries little money. Sports scholarships can be 20%-30% off the quoted school fees. Some scholarships are much less, sometimes just 5% off the full school fees.

If a child is applying for a music scholarship they may be asked to audition by playing a musical piece on their preferred instrument. There is usually stiff competition and what Independent schools are looking for is talent, an interesting child who has a passionate interest in a particular subject, a curious mind and a willingness to excel and be challenged. This is one of the reasons why I regularly advise parents to develop their child's confidence from a young age so that they can appear cool, calm and collected through this gruelling process.

Bursary

Bursaries are usually means tested. This means that before a child qualifies for bursary, there'll be an investigation into the parents' finances to determine eligibility for assistance. The schools usually add a caveat to their application which reads along these lines; "the school reserves the right to seek any other documentary evidence in support of the income and asset figures submitted, and to make enquiries which it deems necessary". Oftentimes, schools will add a warning note such as "We cannot guarantee that every application for support will be successful".

Applicants are usually notified well in advance if their application for financial assistance has been successful. The school Governors determine the value of each bursary award based on information provided by the applicants on their application form. The value of each bursary award can vary and is reviewed annually, taking account of parental circumstances. Parents are advised to budget for an increase in school fees if income goes up. Parents are also advised to notify the school of any changes to their financial circumstances.

A bursary is an amount of money which assists those pupils whose families are not able to afford the school fees. It's usually administered by the bursar, who is the school's business or financial administrator. Bursary applications are highly confidential and parents are advised by schools not to discuss their bursary award with other parents - secrecy again! A number of Independent schools award bursaries to pupils so that they can also maintain their charitable status and pay less tax to the Government. Recently, it was reported that "Three of Scotland's best known Independent schools face losing their charitable status unless they make their fees more affordable for families with lower incomes".
Telegraph (UK) 14 Jan 2013

Outlined below are typical examples of family situations that may attract generous bursaries;

- If a child's parents are employed in roles commanding an income in the region of £18,000-£40,000 or less, with a modest mortgage, the child might receive a 20% discount off the school fees.
- If the parents are earning very low wages and have a mortgage, a child might receive about 40% off the school fees.
- If a child comes from a single parent home with very low income, living in rented accommodation, the child will most likely receive a 100% fee remission.

It is important for parents to bear in mind that schools will consider all their financial circumstances when deciding whether to award a bursary and when they are setting the level of bursary support to award a child. To work out a bursary award, Independent schools usually ask for information about the financial circumstances of parents including all their sources of income, all assets, liabilities and outgoings e.g. child care costs, overdraft payments, loan charges, bills, credit card debts, mortgages, council tax, the number of people in the household etc. This investigation involves checks on parents' bank statements, welfare or state benefits or allowances and mortgage statements. Please note that any income received from letting or subletting of property counts as part of the parental income as well as any dividends received from shares etc. Parents will be asked during the application process if they have any capital that can be released from their savings and investments. The schools go as far as asking if there are other relatives like grandparents who could assist in contributing towards the school fees.

I was advised by a bursar friend of mine that usually, generous bursaries will be awarded to certain families that have an income of less than £15,000 per annum as long as they have not got assets other than the house that they currently occupy. I would advise parents to still apply for the bursary regardless of their financial circumstances. Parents always have the opportunity to speak to the school's bursar to explain their financial circumstances in more detail.

Some Independent schools advertise that parents could be earning about £70,000 a year and still be entitled to some kind of bursary support. There is an understanding that families are facing challenging times financially and that the number of parents applying for assisted places has increased in the last few years. That said, it's not as easy as parents just turning up to an interview with the bursar of the school in an old, rusty, noisy vehicle and pleading severe financial difficulties. Schools don't for a moment look at the outward appearance of their situation; they carry out checks and investigations to ascertain the level of parental income and assets. Parental commitments to the education of other siblings will be considered as well. Where a family has children at other fee-paying schools, it is expected that parents would have made bursary applications to those other schools as well.

I have even heard stories of schools now using the services of Google Earth to check if parents are trying to hide their fast and expensive vehicles which should have been declared as an asset on the bursary application form. A lot of schools are aware that a small fraction of parents fail to declare all the income and assets they have. My advice to parents is to be as open as possible with the bursars so that they don't start their relationship with their child's school with lies.

Educational grants

Some applicants might qualify for grants from charitable trusts that focus on making education more affordable. In some cases parental affiliation to certain societal groups such as the Armed Forces may be a condition to qualify for these grants. In some cases the charitable grant-making trusts can help where there is genuine need. Grants are usually given to help a child complete their current stage of education when parents find themselves in unforeseen financial difficulties. There are several needs recognised by various organisations that award grants. For instance, grants may be awarded in situations where there has been a sudden death of a parent or if a parent suffers from a serious illness. If parents would like to know more about grants they should contact their LEA and also carry out an online search for more information.

Parent Tips:

• If parents know that they are ineligible for financial assistance, it may be helpful and necessary to undertake financial planning to help meet their commitment to the school fees.

• Parents should make the right decision and declare all assets and liabilities. How embarrassing will it be for any parent to get caught out by the school, for lying about their financial capability in order to avoid paying their child's school fees? That's a thought provoking question.

CHAPTER 15

The 'Tiger mum' phenomenon - the role of parents in decision making

Tiger Mum, I am definitely not, but I certainly aspire to be one because I am utterly motivated in trying to ensure that my children attain the best education. This concept is usually associated with the Chinese community. I like the Tiger Mum ideals but I know that I cannot strictly live by the rules. Being a real Tiger Mum involves hours of forced daily music practice and restrictions on extra-curricular activities. Tiger Mums place a total ban on social activities like attending classmates' birthday parties, sleepovers, sports, camps etc. Tiger Mums show more concern for academic excellence. In the last few years, I have tried to adopt some of the principles of this concept in order to maintain discipline and focus. I have excelled in some and failed in others. I will feel bad stopping my kids attending their friends' birthday parties. That said, I agree that the 11+ process requires some elements of 'Tiger Mum discipline'.

The role of parents in the lives and decision-making processes of children is often underestimated. A Tiger Mum is one who does not tolerate mediocrity and has heightened ambition for their child. It's about parents laying the foundation of good work ethics for their child. Tiger Mums don't tolerate any nonsense behaviour from their children and ensure that they operate to the highest academic standards. Although parents love their child, they also need to instil discipline from a young age. Most parents have an element of Tiger Mum in them. Tiger Mums get results!

It's obvious that these days, parents are too afraid of making their children unhappy and don't like to challenge them when they don't for instance wish to do their homework. Over the last few years, I have met a number of children that have exercised total control over their parents. One mother said "little James said he no longer feels like playing the violin anymore so I have stopped his violin tuition".

I asked the parent why she allowed little James to have his way if she as the parent knew that having musical skills is beneficial to him. I was perplexed by this parent's decision. Couldn't this parent have tried harder in encouraging little James to continue learning to play the violin rather than allow him to quit? In my opinion, liberalism is causing more damage than good to families. Parents should be bolder and more forceful in ensuring that their children aim to achieve the highest standards.

As parents, our role is to guide our children in the right way. They are young and they are not always able to make informed judgements. A lot of their decision making process is emotional. My 5 year old said the other day "Mum I wish I could play with my teddy bears all day long and not go to school". Oh! Should I have allowed her to have her way? This is the same scenario that a lot of parents deal with and they fail to exercise the right authority.

It is very important that parents take a leadership but not a dictatorial role on important matters such as choosing the right school and education because this decision will, to a large extent, shape their child's future. I have learnt that there is a fine line between control and discipline.

11+ Revision - Parents be persistent

At the start of my son's 11+ revisions, he displayed a lot of reluctance to his studies and homework. He would hide the homework the tutor gave him and even go to the extent of having temporary amnesia about the set piece of homework given. I panicked about what I perceived to be a lack of seriousness around his 11+ work. However, I was reassured by his tutor who kept telling me that my son would excel. At that stage I felt that the tutor seemed to know my son more than I did. Oh dear! My son also reassured me whenever he saw that I was deeply upset with him. He always had a cheeky grin on his face and at times he would look at me and give a little cheeky wink of an eye.

My son would rather verbalise his thoughts than him write them down. He really did not enjoy Creative Writing. It was a struggle to get two pages of a good story out of him. He was very good in Maths but he just didn't have the patience to check through his work thoroughly for silly mistakes. This was costing him so many marks when I marked his revision papers. I was getting totally frustrated with just months to go before his exams. However, I did not give up. That's the secret to success. Never give up on your child. I learnt that Tiger Mums don't give up until they win. I started to ask the tutor directly for the homework list so that I could get my son to successfully complete all the homework. I continuously heaped praise on his writing skills whenever he wrote a good story. His confidence grew and I saw him blossom in this subject before his 11+ exams.

Parents - watch out for habits affecting a child's performance

At some point during the 11+ revision, I noticed that my son had a really bad habit that was affecting his concentration level. Whenever he sat down, he would start to twist his left ear and would sit in a trance-like state. Obviously it was calming and soothing for him. I noticed that this habit affected his speed level and concentration level. I got worried about this habit as I didn't want this to be the stumbling block to him passing his 11+ exams. Our light bulb moment came when his tutor recommended we buy him ear muffs similar to the one that DJs wear. This helped a lot as my son took his hands away from the ears a lot more. During his 11+ exams, I had to plead with invigilators to allow him to wear these ear muffs as it would help distract him away from twisting his ears for the whole duration of the exams. Thankfully the exam invigilators agreed!

Parent Tips:

- If your child suffers from a habit that may affect them in an exam situation, it is better to stop nagging them about it and try to find a practical solution to the problem. Well, that's what I did and I recommend you do that too. Yelling at a child or punishing them does not always work when it comes to kicking a bad habit. Your decision to get involved in your child's education and prioritise this is very important to their future.

- Never give up on your child. Tiger Mums never do.

CHAPTER 16

My son's experience of a typical 11+ exam day
From one kid to another – kid! Get a grip
Written by Tobi Sangobowale Age 11

"I sat a number of 11+ exams for both Grammar and Independent schools and I was offered a number of school places before I chose to attend my current Grammar school. A typical exam day usually starts with my mum waking me up around 6.00am after having a good night's sleep. I would freshen up, have breakfast and do some last minute revision with my parents. This was mainly about my dear mum trying to drum in important things to remember. After breakfast, my dad and I would set out nice and early for the location of the exam. I love my dad. He accompanied me to every exam I sat. He always got me there on time and I was never late for any exam.

I often saw a lot of children coming in late in a panicked state usually looking very flustered, tearful and confused. I am so happy that I never experienced that. We travelled all over the country for Independent and Grammar school exams.

I usually lay out my favourite clothes the night before and my mum ensured that I packed my bag so that I had at least six pencils, three pens, two erasers, a ruler, a sharpener, my wrist watch and my Maths set. Mum marked my name on all of these items. At times, I had to take identification documents such as my invitation letter from the school, birth certificate and passport photographs to the exam hall.

My experience was the same with most schools that I attended for 11+ exams. There were usually between 400 and 500 other nervous candidates like me sitting the same exams. This usually put a lot of pressure on me and many others. I witnessed a lot of children fall ill on the day of the exams. I did too on one occasion. I was in for some serious competition. On the days of the exams, my dad made sure that I got to the exam hall at least 30 minutes before the start of my exams. In between breaks, the schools gave us snacks in the form of a few biscuits with plenty of water to drink. We usually left the venue around 3pm.

In the week of exams, my parents always made sure that I stayed away from foods such as biscuits, cakes, chocolates and sweets. My mum's explanation is that she didn't want me to take any food that could make me ill before or during my exams. My mum made me drink lots of water to help hydrate my brain".

11+ experience - In the exam hall
"As I walked into the exam halls, I knew that I would be in there for between 3 to 5 hours. In my head, I was trying to remember all the revision I had done. My first exam was Verbal Reasoning with a whooping 80 questions to be answered in 50 minutes.

As I turned over my papers, my heart began beating fast and my pulse began to race. At the same time, I could hear all my mum's wise words ringing in my ears. "Make sure you answer all questions", "make sure you read the instructions", "if you are stuck on one question, move to the next one quickly", "it's about speed and accuracy", "make sure you use your 11+ vocabulary", "use your similes, adjectives and don't forget your punctuation."

Although the atmosphere in the hall was seemingly serious, next to me sat a boy who seemed calm as he sat and tickled the pencil on his desk. I routinely checked the clock which was ahead of me to ensure that it was ticking at the same pace as my wrist watch. I could hear the following words ringing in my head: "Make sure you are conscious of the time." My parents told me this countless times.

Then the invigilators came round to check that all children had put their names and candidate numbers on their answer booklet. Next minute I heard the words, "You have 50 minutes for this test and your time starts now!" These words sent shivers down my spine. I panicked. What If I didn't really know the answers? Time usually flies when you are in these exams. Before I could even say "Jack Robinson", the invigilator shouted the words "TEN MINUTES LEFT" and before I knew it, I heard the invigilator shout out again loudly "YOUR TIME IS UP PLEASE DROP YOUR PENCILS."

I always obey instructions given to me in an exam situation. Again this was one piece of advice my parents always drummed into me. The exam day is usually very nerve wracking and stressful."

A TYPICAL 11+ TEST DAY TIMETABLE

8.50am	Registration
9.30am	Test begins:11+ Mathematics
10.40am	English Comprehension and Grammar
11.15am	Break for 15 minutes
11.40am	Test Begins:11+ Verbal Reasoning
12.40pm	Lunch
1.45pm	English Creative Writing
2.30pm	Non-Verbal Reasoning
3.30pm	End of exams

Rushing through Maths

"I love Maths and enjoy working out the problems really quickly. I always remember my parents saying that I should check my answers over to avoid making silly mistakes. I always take a look at my wrist watch to make sure that I still have enough time to check my work over. I have always been told by my parents from when I was really young that Maths is doable by anyone once you have the basics sorted.

After every exam, I always look forward to my Dad stopping over at a burger place just to give me a lovely treat for the hard work".

Parent Tips:

- If your child is unwell on the day of the exam, please take them to see a doctor either at the hospital or to your local doctor and obtain a doctor's letter. Usually, the school will require evidence that the child has been unwell so that they are given an opportunity to come and sit the papers again. It is advisable for parents not to force their child to sit an exam if they are clearly unwell. There are some schools that are not flexible and will not accept any excuses. If you find yourself in that situation, then clearly, you may have to bundle your child into your car and head off to the exam venue. IF YOUR CHILD IS UNWELL, GET A DOCTOR'S CERTIFICATE!

- A doctor's certificate may be required as proof of mitigating circumstances if a child has to go through the appeals process.

"A dream does not become reality through magic. It takes sweat, determination and hard work"

-Colin Powell

CHAPTER 17
The start of the journey - Having that important pep talk with our child

In 2010, my husband and I sat our then 8 year old son down and had a pep talk with him. We asked him about the secondary school he would like to attend, to which he mentioned the name of one of the local Comprehensive schools near where we live. He had noticed over the years that a number of local children had made a natural progression there. The thought that my son might end up in that particular school gave me shivers and palpitations. Our house sits nicely within the catchment area of the school and the LEA would have offered us this school if we had chosen it on our CAF. Apart from the fact that the school's academic record is questionable in comparison with the national league tables, I have also witnessed the misdemeanours that a number of its pupils get up to outside of the school gates, in the side streets and in the local parks and I felt very worried and panicked.

I then asked my son about his future ambition and he said the following words innocently and loudly "I would really like to be an accountant like Josh (cousin)", "may be a baby doctor like my uncle and also study law like you mum". I was quite happy that he mentioned all these professions. With a smile on my face I replied jokingly "Son, you'll need to go to a really good school that can help you achieve your ambitions".

In my opinion, I just don't think that some Comprehensives deliver what is expected of them and therefore a lot of their pupils suffer academically. However, it's fair to say that I personally know of many pupils that have done exceedingly well in such schools through parental help and support, extra tuition classes, sheer determination and dedication to their studies. I didn't want to dampen my son's spirit by being negative about the local Comprehensive school but I also whispered loudly "it'll be good for you to attend a school that will bring out the best in you".

I shared with him a pictorial image of a school that will really bring out the best in him and boost his confidence. I decided to take him to open days of some Grammar and Independent schools and this is how our 11+ journey began.

Rewards before, during and after the 11+ exam
Prior to my son taking the exam, we had promised him a reward for all the hard work and commitment that he put into the 11+ preparation. He wanted a mobile phone, a pair of Nike trainers and an Arsenal jersey top. He got two out of three. He didn't get the phone but got the others before he got his 11+ results. He worked so hard that it would have been wrong for us to deprive him of a reward. It was well deserved. It's always advisable to offer a reward so that a child will have something to look forward to and something to motivate them. I am aware that some parents give monetary rewards and I don't think there is anything inappropriate about that. It is the parents' responsibility to decide the level of reward to give their child.

General 11+ Exam advice for the exam day

I gave my son a lot of general advice before attending the exams. I am sure I was sounding like a broken record because I kept repeating some of the instructions that I will list below. My son will sometimes look at me; respond with a smile and a mumble of the following words "Mum you have said that before".

Prior to the exams, I told my son the following on a daily basis;

- Never waste too much time on one question. Move quickly to the next question.

- Watch your time and manage it well. Keep an eye on the clock.

- Read the question carefully and follow all instructions.

- Ensure you use the toilet before the exam starts. Avoid going during the exam.

- Ensure that you fill in your name and candidate number on the answer sheet.

- Work through the easy questions first before attempting the tougher questions.

- Make sure you answer every question and try not to guess your answers.

- Go through your exam paper to ensure that you haven't left any question unanswered.

"The roots of education are bitter but the fruit is sweet"

-Aristotle

"Education is the key to unlocking the world, a passport to freedom."

-Oprah Winfrey

CHAPTER 18

After 11+ Exams - Importance Of Year 6 Standard Assessment Tests (SATs)

SATs normally take place in May of when a child is in Year 6. This is usually after they have taken all their 11+ exams. It is important that a child does very well in the SATs tests as the results will be passed to the secondary school that the child will be attending from Year 7. I have met a lot of parents who have told me that SATS results do not really matter. I believe they do matter because some secondary schools use the results to decide on the group set to place the child when they start secondary school.

I am sure it will not help a child's confidence if they start secondary school and suddenly find out that they have been placed in the bottom set in class due to the levels they achieved in their SATs. I would urge parents to encourage their child to work hard in their SATs exams. The Year 7 curriculum is designed to build on students' experience of primary school. It concentrates on developing the key skills for learning which will be used all the way through school and adulthood.

Some schools may use a combination of SATs results and Cognitive Ability Tests[12] (CATs) or their own internal tests to gauge a child's ability. SATs usually cover subjects like Maths, English, a reading test and Science. CATs are used by some schools or LEA to assess a child's Verbal Reasoning skills, Non Verbal Reasoning skills and Maths skills when they start Year 7.

Schools use CATs score to compare the performance of groups of students and for identifying their strengths, weaknesses and target the schools' resources better.

SATS RESULTS – UNDERSTANDING THE LEVELS

SATS Level Comments	Meaning	By Year 6
Level W	Working towards level 1	Very weak
Level 1	Average for a typical 5 year old	weak
Level 2	Average for a typical 7 year old	weak
Level 3	Average for a typical 9 year old	below average
Level 4	Average for a typical 11 year old	good
Level 5	Average for a typical 13 year old	very good
Level 6	Average for a typical 14 year old	very good

Table adapted from SATs guide[13]

It appears as if teachers don't usually like to discuss the levels that children are at in their studies. Parents should endeavour to get this information out of their child's class teacher before it's too late so that if they need to put in some extra work at home, they have enough time to do this before the SATs exams and before a child progresses to Secondary school. A lot of parents don't really want their child to under-perform in their SATs exams.

CHAPTER 19
What if a child does not succeed in 11+?

If parents find themselves in this situation, all hope is not lost. Don't despair. My advice is that parents should ensure that the child does not feel that the parents see them any differently. There are several steps that the parents can take to help their child get through the sticky situation they are in.

Ask the school if the child can be added to the waiting list

Parents are able to ask for feedback from schools directly. It is advisable for parents to just be persistent and not give up easily. This applies most especially to Independent school applications. Parents can request for their child's exam paper to be reviewed and ask for their child to be placed on the waiting list if there is one for their preferred school. Waiting lists quite often can work in a child's favour if other 11+ pupils are removed from the list because they decided to accept admissions from other schools.

Usually, a good number of 11+ candidates apply for places in more than one school. Some would have taken exams for both Independent schools and

Grammar schools. Therefore, there are usually some unforeseen vacancies that can occur in a child's preferred school a few months after the results have been released and places allocated. Keep the faith!

Appeals Process

It is necessary for parents to get familiar with the appeals process of their preferred Grammar schools, Independent schools and the LEA as it is one of the options available when a child is in this desperate situation. The quicker parents act, the better it is. Parents will have to complete and submit the necessary appeal forms which can be obtained from either the preferred school or the LEA. Parents should expect to attend an appeals hearing. Some parents attend the appeals hearing with a representative.

Yearly, a good number of children actually gain admission into Grammar or Independent schools having successfully been through the appeals process. If there are any strong extenuating circumstances such as a recent bereavement, sickness etc that may have caused a child to under-perform in the exams, these reasons are usually tabled before a panel during the appeals process. Sometimes, panels like to see the candidate's Head Teacher's report recommending that the candidate has the ability to succeed in a Grammar School setting. The appeals panels usually consider the strength of the extenuating circumstances that may have caused the loss of marks and they also consider a candidate's overall academic performance.

If the appeals process does not go in the child's favour, parents should not make the child feel as if they will never achieve their ambition in life. Parents need to be careful not to use hurtful words as these could stick on their mind for a very long time and damage their confidence. Parents should make sure that they continue to encourage their child. Speak positive words to them. This is not the time to start to tell all the uncles and aunties that they failed. It is important to be sensitive to the child's feelings. The parents' actions may affect them for the rest of their lives so please show kindness to them. Anger is a normal reaction which needs to be controlled and it is a non-productive emotion. There are still other options to consider as outlined in the following paragraphs.

12+ and 13+ Exams

There is the opportunity to sit subsequent exams such as 12+ and 13+ Common Entrance Exams for entry to year 8 and Year 9 of some Grammar and Independent schools. It's not all schools that provide this option therefore, Parents will have to carry out a research of the schools that follow this process and ensure that the child continue to make adequate preparation towards these exams.

Organise extra tuition for the child

If a child's only feasible option is to attend a non-performing comprehensive school, then parents must ensure that they continue to encourage the child to work very hard so that they can achieve good grades in their GCSEs. Parents must try their best to ensure that they budget for private tuition for their child especially in the English, Maths and science subjects. This will certainly go a long way and will help the child succeed against all odds. Many children excel in Comprehensive schools through sheer hard work and determination.

Home–schooling

I know of some situations whereby parents decided not to send their child to the non-performing comprehensive school allocated to them by the LEA but instead chose to keep their child ahead of school educated peers by home schooling. Parents in this situation normally make use of a combination of really good textbooks, online resources and personal tutors. Some parents also go for this option anticipating that their child will quickly move up the waiting list of their preferred school.

I hope that I can put some parents' minds at rest by saying Relax! Encourage your child to continue to work hard and believe in themselves.

Attend sixth form at a Grammar school or an Independent school

A good number of Grammar and Independent schools accept sixth form A'levels applications from candidates that have attended Comprehensive schools. This stage is the last stage of secondary education for pupils that attend sixth form. Although their admissions criteria are usually very high, I would advise that a child considering this option must ensure that they get exceptionally good GCSE grades and parents should ensure they familiarise themselves with the admissions criteria of the Grammar or Independent school being considered.

Parent Tip: If a child does not pass their 11+; it's not the end of the world. Please do not nag them or damage their confidence. Give them constant re-assurance that they will have a bright future in any school they attend as long as they work extremely hard and take their studies seriously. Ensure you arrange for extra tuition if necessary to help with any subject in which your child lacks confidence.

CHAPTER 20
Poetry: 'The boy named TY'
By Tobi Sangobowale

There once was a boy named Ty

Who always looked up to the sky,

Who once went to play,

For the rest of the day,

But then saw a door

And was curious what it was for.

Ty crossed the door line,

And thought everything was fine,

But in his presence stood a mountain,

On top of which, stood a victory fountain,

Ty started to hike the mountain,

To get to the special fountain.

When Ty got to the top,

He started to dance and body pop,

Ty just remembered the tremendous fountain,

That stood on top of the humongous mountain.

As he drank the powerful water,

He started to feel even stronger,

He started to hike down,

For his mother was waiting for him with a frown,

Ty was an hour late for his tea,

But he was grateful because for once he felt free.

Some useful websites

There are a number of websites that offer really useful information on the 11+ exams and a few of these have been listed below. This list is by no means exhaustive. I would urge parents to please continue to carry out their research for any other pieces of information that will help develop their child's future.

1. http://www.aetuition.co.uk/
2. www.bbc.co.uk - for information on schools League Tables
3. www.bond11plus.co.uk - for free revision papers and exam tips
4. http://www.cem.org/ - for more information on CEM 11+ tests
5. http://www.chuckra.co.uk/ - for free resources and online practice papers
6. www.elevenplusexams.co.uk -parents' forum
7. http://www.galorepark.co.uk/- publisher of educational textbooks for pupils studying at Independent schools
8. www.google.com - if all fails use this search engine to search for any information you require
9. http://www.grammar-monster.com/ - for help with grammar, punctuation and vocabulary
10. www.Independent.co.uk - for information on top Independent and Grammar schools at A'levels and GCSEs and top 100 selective schools in the UK
11. http://www.iseb.co.uk/ - for more information on Independent schools' 11+ exams
12. http://www.nelsonthornes.com/shop/nt/bond-11-plus- to purchase bond 11+ books
13. http://www.ngsa.org.uk/faqs.php - for information about Grammar Schools
14. http://www.satsguide.co.uk/what_are_sats.htm
15. http://www.11plus.co.uk – for free resources and online practice papers
16. www.britishcouncil.org – Find information for international students that want to study in the United Kingdom.

(Endnotes)

1. The Consortium consists of a group of selective schools with the objective of participating in a common activity which is the 11+ exams. These schools pool their resources for achieving a common goal. They save pupils from having to take multiple tests. Instead pupils sit one exam for admission into the Grammar schools in the consortium.

(Endnotes)

1. OFSTED (Office for Standards in Education)

2. National Grammar Schools Association's website
    http://www.ngsa.org.uk/

3. State-funded schools are schools whose main funding comes from either local Government or the central Government through Taxation. State funded schools usually follow the same National curriculum.

4. "Admission to State Boarding Schools in the UK is limited to children who are nationals of the UK and are eligible to hold a full UK passport, or those who are nationals of other European Union countries or those who have the right of residence in the UK"-source http://www.sbsa.org.uk/

5. Information and Communications Technology

6. The Russell Group universities are often described as "elite". There are 24 institutions in this group and they carry out some of the most highly rated research in the world and have a reputation for academic excellence. They have higher than average student satisfaction and lower than average drop-out rates, according to research. The Russell Group was formed in 1994 by 17 British research universities - Birmingham, Bristol, Cambridge, Edinburgh, Glasgow, Imperial College London, Leeds, Liverpool, London School of Economics, Manchester, Newcastle, Nottingham, Oxford, Sheffield, Southampton, University College London and Warwick. In 1998

Cardiff University and King's College London joined the group.

7. The term Ivy League commonly refers to a group of eight private, colleges and universities in the United States of America renowned for providing an excellent education. The universities in this category are Harvard, Yale, Pennsylvania, Princeton, Columbia, Brown, Dartmouth and Cornell. Ivy League schools are viewed as some of the most prestigious, and are ranked among the best universities worldwide.

8. Duke of Edinburgh's award website is http://www.dofe.org/

9. Standard Assessment tests are compulsory national tests that primary school pupils are required to take at the ages of 6-7 (Key Stage 1) and at ages 10-11 (Key Stage 2).

10. This is an adapted 11+ timetable for one of the Independent schools in the UK.

11. The National Offer Day is the day that Year 6 pupils all over the UK find out which secondary schools they have been allocated by their LEA. Places are allocated at the beginning of March following applications submitted by parents in the autumn term of Year 6.

12. Most secondary schools use CATs, to assess a pupil's ability in Verbal Reasoning ; Numerical reasoning and Non-Verbal Reasoning

13. http://www.satsguide.co.uk/what_are_sats.htm

List of Abbreviations

CAF	Common Application Form
CAT	Cognitive Ability Tests
CEM	Centre for Evaluation and Monitoring
ICT	Information and Communications Technology
ISEB	Independent Schools Examination Board
LEA	Local Education Authority
NON-VR / NVR	Non Verbal Reasoning
OFSTED	Office for Standards in Education
SATs	Standard Assessment Tests
SIF	Supplementary Information Form
VR	Verbal Reasoning

I value your feedback and want to hear your thoughts, comments and suggestions about this book.

Please send your comments and feedback to parentsgetagrip@hotmail.com or visit www.getthegrip.co.uk

Lightning Source UK Ltd.
Milton Keynes UK
UKOW02f1447070716

277885UK00002B/83/P